What others

I have built a 6-figure fitness business with a team of trainers and on my way to unlocking the $250,000 a year club which, with the help of Jason, I know I will hit! Not only have learnt intense sales and marketing but most importantly the psychology and how to really connect with people.

Daniel Rousso – Melbourne Australia

With the help of Jason Grossman ... I have been able to grow my online fitness business to 6-figures, to the stage where I am so busy that I now employ 2 more coaches to help with the demand, a telemarketer to manage the abundance of leads, and am leveraging even more through my menopause program for PT's.

Lyn Miller – Gold Coast Australia

...if it wasn't for Simon, Jason and the QFM team, I would not have had the belief and tools necessary to realize my dream. I am eternally grateful, and I will go all the way to the top with QFM to the millionaires' group and beyond. I have 3 years to be a millionaire by the time I am 30.

Tiarnán Carlin – England, United Kingdom

Contacting Quantum Fitness Marketing was the best decision I have made for my business to date. Without Jason and Rhys' help, I would be just another passionate fitness pro chasing my tail in the business world, not maximizing my potential.

Jenna May – Adelaide, Australia

Although I have been in the industry for many more years than Simon, and even Jason, these guys had moved on in the industry. Businesswise they have tools that I did not even know existed for PT businesses! Thanks, Simon and Jason, for your coaching and support, very grateful!

Rod Fielder – Auckland, New Zealand

If you are reading this and have never tried having a business coach to take it to the next level, then I highly recommend you give it a go! It's been the best thing I have ever done, and I am now living my destiny and doing what I was born to do.

James Trenow – Perth, Western Australia

I came across Jason and Quantum Fitness Marketing on Facebook and arranged our first coaching call. 18 months on, with the guidance of Jason, I have built a team of 5 trainers all across Adelaide, and I am currently making more than 250k per year! I was also lucky enough to become a business coach for QFM, and I am now helping personal trainers in 4 countries as their business coach to follow their dreams and our systems to build to 6-figures plus.

Lachy Black – Adelaide, Australia

Finding Jason and joining this amazing community has completely revolutionized my life ... Through his program and guidance, I was able to build to 100k a year income in just 4 weeks after joining a big box gym! This absolutely blew my mind that it could be done so fast. With my sights set on success, I continued to build.

Rhys Margan – Perth, Western Australia

Anything is possible, and if you ever get the chance to read this and are thinking about making a decision to make your fitness business explode, then you are certainly in the right place.

Simon Finch – Melbourne, Australia

With Jason striving to make all those who follow him a millionaire, I jumped in completely open minded and ready to learn ... From there my business became a rocket ship. I was being provided strategies that I had never even considered—strategies not only for my business but for me personally. I was provided the tools and mindset to take financial control of my life. Before I knew it, I achieved my 500k badge with my sights now set on accomplishing a million-dollar-a-year fitness business.

Dustin Wenzel – Michigan, United States of America

See *Extended Testimonials* at the back of the book
for the full stories from each of these Personal Trainers.

THE PERSONAL TRAINING BUSINESS BIBLE

HOW TO BUILD A 6 THEN 7 FIGURE FITNESS BUSINESS

JASON GROSSMAN

Copyright © 2018 Jason Grossman

ISBN: 978-1-925681-85-7

Published by Vivid Publishing
P.O. Box 948, Fremantle
Western Australia 6959
www.vividpublishing.com.au

Cataloguing-in-Publication data is available from the National Library of Australia

Table of Contents

BONUS CHAPTERS

1

INTRODUCTION

Thank you for your trust and taking the time to purchase then read this book. Congratulations on your commitment to excelling in your fitness business and creating something extraordinary. After 18 years in the fitness industry, I have never created anything quite like this. A simple yet powerful blueprint for the fitness business owner who is ambitious, hungry and wanting more from life. A fitness business owner who doesn't merely want to survive, but wants to thrive. Who does not want simply to get booked solid, but rather, who wants to build a large fitness business and impact even more lives.

You may be new to the industry or even a veteran. You may be a rental trainer, studio owner or mobile trainer. Regardless of the style of business you currently operate (if at all), I'm going to share with you my personal experience, how I spent a decade as a 6-figure trainer. Then personally built multiple 7-figure fitness businesses. I've also been involved hands-on with building over 1200 fitness businesses from 11 countries to 6, 7 and multiple 7 figures.

I know for some it may seem a little pie in the sky, or unrealistic.

But all I know is, if someone else can do it, so can I. And If I, a high school dropout, can do it—so too can you!

Unfortunately, around 80% of fitness business owners only earn an average of around $1000 dollars gross, give or take, a week. This is barely enough to survive on, let alone thrive on. Then the 'successful' trainers book themselves solid, stay there for 5-10 years, and burn out. This 'was' me… I spent almost a decade delivering 60-80 sessions week in, week out, and burnt out. I was diagnosed with glandular fever, then chronic fatigue. I wouldn't wish that upon anyone!

I don't claim to have all the answers, and this is not gospel, though it is called a bible. It's simply a handbook and manual that shares my personal experience over the past 18 years of being a part of building over 1200 fitness businesses, and the strategies I have learned along the way.

Some people may believe it's not possible or it is unrealistic to achieve a 7-figure fitness business. I can understand and appreciate that; however, the first step in achieving a 7-figure fitness business is to believe that it's possible, that you are capable, and you deserve it. Even though the sub-title of this book is a monetary title, to be honest, this is not about the money at all. Rather, it's about the ability to raise your standards to impact many more lives, and in the process, create the life you dream of. My goal is not just to show you how to build a successful fitness business; it's to show you how to create the business that supports the life you dream of.

In fact, that is my mission with this book, to show you exactly how, step by step, you can build the business that creates financial freedom for you and your family to live the lifestyle you dream of. All while impacting many more lives. If you aim small, you hit small. If you aim large, you hit large.

I don't just want you to book solid, I want you to be free. Free from the stress and worry of money and a lack of time.

Mediocrity is not measured in comparison to anyone else, it's when you settle for a life that is less than the one you are capable of living. I truly do believe in you and that you have greatness in you. As you begin to read this book front to back, if you read with an open mind, and not only absorb the information like a sponge, but also apply the strategies in this book, you too can create a 7-figure fitness business, creating the life of your dreams.

You have an untouched, unlimited reservoir of pure potentiality, and if you can choose to tap into it, harness it, and unleash it upon the world, you can achieve anything. But you must believe in yourself and back yourself with the right plan, people, and actions, so you can create the fitness business and life of your dreams.

As you read this entire book, you will discover within these pages the exact steps you can begin to take to create a work-life balance, and build a 7-figure fitness business and beyond. You will also discover the psychology of business and unravel some mental blockages that may have been holding you back.

In this book, I will guide you step by step to build a 6-figure fitness business, then a quarter of a million dollar-a-year fitness business, then 7 figures and beyond. So regardless of where you are currently at with building your fitness business, this book has what you need to achieve your fitness business goals.

If you are a brand-new Personal Trainer (PT), recently qualified, then this book will show you how to build from where you are right now, step-by-step to 6 figures ($2000 a week)! If you have been a PT for a while and are already making 6 figures, this book will show you how to build a consistent income to $250,000 a year. If you already are making $250,000 a year, and have a reasonable size fitness business, this book will show you with specific steps how to build to 7 figures, then beyond. You will scale your fitness business and align your psychology for success along the way.

If you read this entire book from front to back with an open mind, and apply the tools and techniques within these pages, it's not just possible for you to create a 7-figure fitness business, it's highly probable.

So, I want to challenge you right now, as you continue reading this, to put all your old limiting beliefs aside, to think with abundance, possibility, and an open mind. To put your past experiences behind you. I challenge you to raise your standards and play a bigger game, so you can be more, do more, and give more.

As we get ready to embark upon this journey together, know that this book is not only a road map for you to follow, with sales, marketing, systems and more to build your PT business. There are also five bonus chapters at the end specifically focused on other modalities and business models for fitness business owners, including Online PT, bootcamp, semi-private, and studio owners.

I understand that in addition to PT, there is a good chance you are using one of these services, and since this book is titled a bible, a complete manual of sorts, I wanted to make this a comprehensive manual for all fitness business owners.

Finally, the very last bonus chapter has a ton of cool resources you can use to build your business and add even more value to you!

So, if you are ready and hungry for more, let's begin....

2

MY PERSONAL STORY

When I was a young child, my mother and father, who were quite young themselves, separated and got divorced. I don't remember the ordeal, but I do remember what it was like not long after, when Mum remarried to a man who was violent towards her on a regular basis. Soon they too were divorced, and afterwards, he set a bonfire and burnt everything, including pretty much all my baby and child photos (I have only half a dozen now). We moved into a women's refuge to go into hiding. I was now the man of the house, just a child, and the eldest of four.

Around that time is a bit of a blur for me, I'm guessing for obvious reasons, but after a bunch of physical ordeals and dramas we moved to a suburb called Lockridge in Perth, Western Australia. At the time, it was the roughest suburb in Western Australia, full of government housing, flats and units. I was quite a chubby kid who didn't seem to fit in and got picked on a lot because of it, so I became a bully. I remember getting into fights almost daily, including an ordeal with scissors.

Before too long I was in high school and that's when the fun began.

The very first week at our school (the roughest in Western Australia), there was another kid that got stabbed repeatedly. It wasn't long before I was going to parties and smoking marijuana and drinking alcohol. We used to even buy casks of wine and smoke joints on our lunch breaks. We would even drink the casks of wine at the back of the class in school.

By year ten it was the norm to carry a knife for protection, as there were fights most days, and stabbings were common occurrences, and I even recall a few shootings. I was stabbed, hit in the back of the head with a sledgehammer, and hit in the face with the back of an axe, all before the age of sixteen, when I was kicked out of home. That was when my mum told me that she was dying of cancer, and we found out that she had severe bipolar disorder. Now I was homeless, a high school dropout.

Once I got kicked out I started staying at different friends' houses until I outstayed my welcome, and my next option was youth hostels. That was when I started getting into more serious drugs including Rohypnol, pills, speed and ecstasy. Within six months, due to many issues I had caused within the hostels, I was banned from every hostel in Perth, and had nowhere to stay but the streets, parks and any other place I could find in Perth where I wouldn't get arrested. I literally only had the clothes on my back and sometimes would go for days without food. I would beg for money, but would spend it on alcohol. After six months on the streets I was introduced to heroin, and it was over the next twelve months that I got a real wake-up call. I now had a new circle of friends and they were all heroin addicts. I remember some days shooting up $1000 worth of heroin, and I am sure you can guess where the money came from. That year I had many friends die from overdoses and car accidents, as well as being in a severe car accident myself, plus getting hit by a car.

By that stage I had been arrested or locked up around a dozen times for myriad things, and had overdosed twice. The third time I overdosed I died for a moment, and they thought they had lost me. I knew that was the last straw, and that I would end up dead or in prison if I didn't turn my life around. Once released from hospital I had nowhere to stay, so I rang my mum (who was in her third marriage), and took refuge with her so I could clean up and detox. The first day wasn't so bad, the second was hard, and by the third I was shaking, having cold sweats, and delusional (what you see in the movies is no exaggeration). I managed to get a few Temazepam (valium) from my mum to help, but then ended up stealing the entire bottle and taking all fifty of them. I then went a little ballistic with an axe on the street (not knowing what I was doing), chopping at anything in sight. My mum's husband had threatened to shoot me, as he used to hunt. I remember running straight for them at the door with the axe as they went inside. I went to start chopping at the door. Then I turned to the left and saw my sister with her face pressed against the window, fearful and in tears.

I came to, dropped the axe and fell to my knees crying—I had never cried so much in my life—until the police came, and I spent three nights in lock up, which forced me to detox. I had three whole days in solitude to think about my life. I was sad, then angry. I always felt from a young age that I was meant to do great things, that I was special, that I could make a difference in this world by leaving a legacy, but I had been doing the opposite. After that, I committed myself and set my mind to being the best I could be and to giving back to society. But we all know that it takes time to really shift one's character, personality, habits and beliefs at the unconscious level.

Once I was released, I spent a few days on a park bench with a pen and paper creating my plan. I was going to find a shared place to live, get a job and get into martial arts. So, within a month of detoxing I had done all of these things. Just four weeks before this I was at a crossroads, to die, go to prison, or fight for what I knew I could be. Do and have. It was hard, but I began spending a lot of my time with martial arts and reading books about psychology to understand how the mind works. There were several relapses over the year, but nothing too serious. I decided to do my personal training course, and then got a job as a PT. PT LITERALLY got me of the streets, saved my life and kept me off the streets. Within just nine months I was the busiest personal trainer in Western Australia, and one of the busiest in Australia with a 6-figure PT Business at just 22 years of age.

Many PTs asked how I managed to book 80-100 sessions every week so fast. To be honest, I was just crazy hungry. I didn't have any sales training yet, but I figured if the gym was open then I would be there seven days a week being seen. I also made sure I never walked past someone more than twice without finding out their name and striking up a conversation. I will share more of my fitness business story later in this book.

After doing PT, my learning obsession grew, and I studied business, and it wasn't until I came across the therapy NLP (neuro-linguistic programming) that I was truly able to overcome my demons. I was ashamed and couldn't talk about my past, so I found youth and people I could share my story with in the hope to inspire them, while I used NLP to overcome my demons, which I can gladly say I have.

After nine years of PT and other health and wellness businesses, I realized it was time for me to step up, so I started coaching Personal Trainers to grow their own businesses. My passions were business, health and fitness so it made sense. Next thing I knew, we were operating a 7-figure health and fitness company with 17 amazing staff members, helping to change lives worldwide through nutrition, coaching, health education, personal training, and more, including working with charity organizations to make a difference and creating a million-dollar business.

Growing a large business and truly making a difference can be hard work, as you need resilience, internal fortitude, patience, and the ability to overcome adversity. If it wasn't for my past experiences, I truly believe that I wouldn't be doing what I am today.

BUT THEN ... I went and did something crazy. Early in 2012, I fell madly in love with my sweetheart Kailey, the woman of my dreams. Next thing I knew I was closing my company, and gave all my belongings away to my family and charity. I then moved from Perth to Brisbane (west coast to east coast) Australia to be with her. All with just a suitcase, $218,000 debt and an income of $297 a week.

I decided this time I wanted to set up a business that not only created a healthy happy lifestyle for others anywhere in the world, but also allowed me to live mine. I had built a 7-figure business in 18 months before, so surely, I could do it again.

So, this time in just nine months I built a 7-figure business completely online from scratch. Two-and-a-half years later, we had a team of almost 70 from across the globe, helping people create happier, healthier lifestyles through nutrition, fitness, mindset, lifestyle design, financial freedom, charity, and more. We included online personal training, business coaching, life coaching, lifestyle design, and a bunch of amazing programs, products and services, all to take us closer, step by step, to achieving our mission to help create one million happier and healthier lives!

Kailey and I recently spent two-and-a-half years straight travelling to eighteen countries and ticking off over 240 bucket list items, and now wherever we are, we can run our online businesses with a multi-million-dollar turnover, do live events, and change lives, living our dream life through lifestyle design! Because of this, we are also able to build a portfolio of properties and gyms, and invest in other businesses.

Helping people turn their dreams into reality is my true passion, as corny as it sounds, because it is possible if you make the choice.

I share this not to impress you but to impress upon you, so that you can see that no matter who you are, where you come from, or what adversity you face, it's not how hard you get hit, but how you get up with a vengeance. And in the words of Eminem, 'to not give up and not be a quitter' because you are special, and you can do great things. You have an untapped abundant reservoir of potential that, once you tap into it, will surprise even yourself.

3

THE PSYCHOLOGY OF A SUCCESSFUL FITNESS BUSINESS OWNER

If you were to give a client a world class meal plan and fitness plan, would that guarantee their results? Probably not, right?

Why is that? Many people would agree it's because if the mindset is not congruent, there may be limiting beliefs, values, habits, thoughts and self-sabotage holding people back. Even if I was to give you the recipe to build a 6- then 7-figure fitness business, does that guarantee you will? Probably not. Some experts say 80% of success is psychology and 20% is mechanics. I like to say 77% of all statistics are made up—ha! I'm not sure what the percentage is, but I'm sure we can agree that mind set plays a much larger role than anything in the external world.

I also believe that we don't become successful, we attract success by the person we become. Although most fitness business owners are barely getting by, there are a few that are crushing it. I truly believe the main reason is their psychology.

In order to build a 6-, then 7-figure fitness business, we want to think, act, believe, and perceive like a 7-figure business owner.

So, what's Is the mind set necessary for building a 6- then 7-figure fitness business?

Let's take a look, shall we...

THE POWER OF BELIEF

The first step many say is the hardest. Before giving you the strategy necessary to build a 6- then 7-figure fitness business, you must believe that it's possible, you deserve it, and you are capable. It is ten times more powerful and important to believe it's possible, than to understand how to do it. Because doubt is a dream killer. It leads to procrastination, self-sabotage, and inaction. You need to know in your heart of hearts you can do it because someone else has.

To believe 100% that you are deserving of it and 100% you are capable of building a 6- then 7-figure fitness business is the very first step. If I, a high school dropout, can do it, so too can you. I understand most fitness business owners fail and definitely don't have this level of success—but why not you?

As you read this, you may be thinking, that's great Jason, but I'm not sure I do have that 100% faith and believe. So how do I truly believe it at the unconscious level?

1. **Desire:** You must have an unwavering desire, a hunger that almost becomes a magnificent obsession. A healthy obsession that is built on a strong *why*, and a personal mission. It's not enough to simply want a 6- then 7-figure business—you must know *why* you want it. The first thing you think of when you jump out of bed, the last thing you think of before going to sleep, is your outcome, which is defined by your *why*. Take a moment to write down *why* it truly is important for you, and *why* you must achieve a 6- then 7-figure fitness business.

2. **Proximity:** Proximity is power. Who you hang out with truly does influence the success or lack of it in your own life. The problem is, most trainers are struggling, most businesses do fail. So, it's very important we associate with people who are winning. Other fitness business owners that have momentum and are on track for building a 6- then 7-figure fitness business, and also people that are already running a 6- then 7-figure fitness business. This is so important. There literally are no words to explain just how big this truly is. If you don't have a coach or mentor yet, now is the time.

3. **Skill:** Jim Rohn used to say, don't wish life was easier, wish you were better, don't wish for less problems, wish for more skills. Don't wish building a business was easier, wish you were better at it. Study every day, for thirty minutes to an hour, marketing, sales, business systems, and master your craft. Attend seminars and courses, listen to personal development audios, and every day, become just that little bit better until you gain unconscious competence.

4. **Momentum:** Building a business is like a strong man truck-pull competition. You know, when the strong man has a harness and rope attached to his waist then to a truck. The truck is stationary and he must get the truck moving, so he gets nice and low, and exerts 100% of his energy to take the first step, which is the hardest; with each step he takes, the truck gains more and more momentum, and it gets easier and easier, to the point when he can easily walk across the finish line and the truck will continue to roll without him. Your business is the same. It gets easier as you gain momentum. And as you gain momentum and see more results, it will boost your confidence and belief.

So you form a magnificent obsession about your goal and why you want it. Associate with people who are already doing what you want. Study daily, and build momentum. Your belief will sky rocket faster than you can ever imagine. I see it all the time!

Additionally, you can create a vision board, and place the graphics below on it. Look at them every morning and every night, keeping it in your mind's eye. Every morning and evening, visualize and imagine, looking through your own eyes, having already built a 6- and/or 7-figure fitness business. Notice what you can see, hear and feel. And then increase those feelings. Form a magnificent obsession. Let those thoughts dominate your mind, not for the money, but for the lives impacted on the journey!

IT STARTS WITH A DECISION

Have you ever had a client that just didn't seem to be committed? They would miss sessions, forget their diary, and be inconsistent? Have you ever tried to change a habit but it didn't seem to happen? When I was a teenager living on the streets as a heroin addict, it took me multiple times to finally stop heroin for good. In fact, I overdosed three times, and the third time I was clinically dead for nearly three minutes. It wasn't until I said to myself, enough is enough, and made a hundred percent decision to make a change because I had to, that I committed to my goal. Now you are forming your belief, for you to succeed, you need to make a decision. If you truly want to build a 6- then 7-figure fitness business and your why is built on changing lives and helping people, including yourself, you need to make a decision *right now* that you are going to win. That you are prepared to do whatever it takes UNTIL you succeed. UNTIL you win. You become an UNTIL person UNTIL you reach your goal. No excuses!!! You may not know how, you may not know when, but that doesn't matter, because if you decide right now you are going to pursue this dream until it happens, then it's a done deal. Once you make this decision the only way you can truly fail is to quit. You're not a quitter, are you? You are a champion, a winner! So, I challenge you right now to decide to win, because you are capable, and you do deserve it. That you are going to do whatever it takes for as long as it takes to make this work and you are all in. There is no retreat and no surrender. You must make this happen because…

Answer this question: I decide to win now because….?

DOUBT

The very moment you make a decision to make a change, a voice will appear inside your mind and start to pre-judge: I don't know how to do that. How do I do that? Is it even possible? Etcetera. You know the voice I'm talking about? Yes, that's the one right there!

That's simply the brain's physiological response to not wanting to change; its number one role is a protective mechanism. It knows once you make a decision to create change, along that journey will be setbacks and failures which will lead to pain. Also, the brain likes familiarity, it likes comfort, it doesn't want to create new neural pathways. So, in future when you do hear that voice, you will simply remember that that means you are actually on track for creating the change you desire.

One of those voices you will hear is the voice of doubt. Hearing the voice of doubt makes you human, it's a natural response. Hearing the voice of doubt is a given, BUT acting on it or not is a choice. The more you condition yourself to hear the voice of doubt and take action anyway, the more successful you will be. It's natural for you to hear the voices of doubt, so don't think there is something wrong with you, or you are different. It has nothing to do with skill, capability or confidence, it's simply the brain trying to trick you into staying the same. Don't let your brain run you. Instead tell your brain to shut up, sit down, and that you got this.

I often say the key to success is turning your brain off, and turning your hands on. Once I make a decision I often don't think about it much, unless it's focused on the attainment of that outcome, and stated and visualized positively. As Tony Robbins says, I see things how they are, but then I see them better than they are!

The best way I have found to condition myself to hear the voice of doubt and take action anyway is to put myself in uncomfortable situations on a very regular basis. To have new experiences that create new learnings and lead to more curiosity. Become obsessed with learning and growth. Knowing that mistakes are good because there can be no learning without mistakes. We either WIN or we LEARN! We begin to enjoy the learning process, and understand that mistakes and doubt are a natural part of growth, which cannot exist without those experiences.

FEAR

Fear is very similar to doubt; it just feels MUCH more intense. We have heard things like: FEAR is simply False Evidence Appearing Real, and FEAR is Forget Everything And Run, or Face Everything And Rise. Fear is not a bad thing; we need fear to protect us against harm. However, there are times fear can really hold us back from achieving our dreams. Cognitively, when we think, our thoughts will determine how we feel, how we feel will determine our actions, and our actions will determine our outcomes. (In my book, *From the Streets to a Millionaire*, I go more in-depth about these mind cycles.) BUT we can choose our responses between each of these steps. We can choose what we think, which will determine how we feel; we can choose our actions, which will determine our outcomes. We don't have to be slaves to conditioning based on who we believe we are. We can change and be anything or anyone we choose.

We may never truly eliminate fear, as courage isn't the absence of fear, it's having the fear and taking action anyway. The key is to condition yourself to feel the fear and take action anyway. The more you do this, fear itself will actually become a trigger to act. I strongly suggest writing down your biggest fear right now, then facing it within the next fourteen days, because if you can do that, then you can do anything, and that includes building a 7-figure fitness business. This is why I love doing adrenaline activities; it still scares the hell out of me, but I'm showing my brain who is boss. It doesn't matter if I'm scared, I'm still going to do it no matter what because of how I will feel if I do face my fear, and what it will mean for me if I don't. If nothing changes, nothing changes! Be brave, bold and do something in the next fourteen days you have never considered doing, then make it a part of your rituals.

CONGRUITY

Without congruity, there can never be success. Even if you believe it, make a decision, hear the doubt and feel the fear, and take action anyway, if you do not align these three things you will never be successful AND fulfilled.

Congruity is when we align or thoughts, feelings and actions. What does this mean?

It means that if you are thinking about a 6- or 7-figure fitness business, and you are feeling excited by it but you are not taking the action in this book, you will not achieve a 6- or a 7-figure fitness business.

It means if you are thinking about a 6- or 7-figure fitness business and you are feeling anxious or stressed about it, even if you take the action in this book, you will not be successful.

It means If you are not focused on or thinking enough about building a 6- or 7-figure fitness business, but you are taking the steps in this book and even feeling good about it, you will still not succeed.

Success comes when we focus on what we want consistently multiple times a day, we are feeling certain and positive about it, excited even, and we are taking massive action daily towards its attainment. That's what will create success for you in any area of life.

Begin to notice how you are thinking and feeling. If you are thinking or feeling in an incongruent way, start to take the time to switch your focus and your physiology to align these three elements.

MENTAL VITAMINS

Our mind is like a garden. A garden has beautiful flowers and it can also grow weeds. In order to keep the weeds out we need to cultivate our garden on a regular basis. Our mind can have positive thoughts and negative. And if we don't consciously weed the negative thoughts from our mind, like weeds, they can be destructive. Below, I have outlined what I call the five mental vitamins, with which, if you take them daily, you can keep your mind free of negative thoughts and begin to align your psychology for success. I call it becoming an athlete of the mind. They are very simple, and things you probably know, but do you apply them in your everyday life?

VITAMIN A - ABANDON ALL EXCUSES

Sounds pretty simple, right? Abandon all excuses?

An athlete of the mind that shapes their own life and destiny makes no excuses. They take full responsibility for their own life. They understand that everything that happens in their life is because of the choices they make and the actions they take. Their thoughts, fears, beliefs, values, and feelings shape their world. Their actions, speech, behaviour, and habits are what gives them everything they have in their life.

Not the government, not the economy, not the weather, not their parents. The athlete of the mind who takes vitamin A every day understands that for everything that happens in our life, we have a window of opportunity to decide and choose our response. We don't have to simply react by default or conditioning. The athlete of the mind understands that we have a response-ability—the ability to choose to respond and shift and control the outcomes in our everyday life.

VITAMIN B - BECOME AN 'UNTIL' PERSON

Become an until person and commit to doing whatever it takes until your dreams become a reality, and you can never truly fail!
— Jason Grossman

An until person doesn't say, 'well I gave it my best'. An until person doesn't make excuses. An until person does whatever it takes until they achieve their goals. They eliminate the word 'if' and replace it with the word 'when'.

An until person is prepared to do whatever it takes until their dreams become a reality. An until person takes full responsibility for everything in their life.

Have you ever noticed that truly fulfilled, happy and successful people seem to have that cheeky smile, you know, the one that oozes confidence? Ever wondered why that is? It's almost like they know something you don't. Well, it's because they are an until person.

When we are young, many of us are told not to expect things, things don't come for free. We hear the word 'no' a lot; work hard, go get a job, get an education and don't expect things.

The stonecutter takes a hammer and hits a large stone with great force in the right spot, and ... gets no result. He hits again and again. After possibly hundreds of hits, the stone finally breaks. The cutter keeps going with the knowledge that he WILL get the desired result, because he will not stop striking the stone with his hammer UNTIL it cracks. Some people have characters that have a bit of granite in them. Do you?

It's NOT Over Until You Win

— Les Brown

VITAMIN C - COURAGEOUSLY ACT UPON YOUR DREAMS

Courage is going from failure to failure without losing enthusiasm.
— Winston Churchill

When you set goals, work towards your dreams and build your fitness business, you will feel uncertain at times, and you will have fears. It's only natural; you are about to embark upon a journey you've never experienced before. You are about to step into the unknown, and for many the unknown can be scary.

Many people talk about the fear of failure, but what about fear of success?

What if I become rich, will people think less of me?
What if I become famous, will that change me into someone I don't like?
Will I lose loved ones?
Will people ask me for money?
What will it really mean for me?

It's really the fear of the unknown, which many say is the biggest fear of all. You can never really know until you give it a go and you arrive. By aligning and staying true to your values, focusing on adding value and asking what you will give, you will find many of these fears dissipate and even completely disappear. Remember that courage isn't the absence of fear; it is having the fear and taking action anyway! Ask yourself, does this action help others? Is it with good intention? Am I in alignment with my values?

If yes, then you know you are on the right path. Life is more meaningful when you make it about giving and leaving a legacy. Forget about the money and success, focus on gratitude and contribution, and feel the fear, doubt and uncertainty melt away. An athlete of the mind feels the fear, then acts anyway. They understand that the more they feel the fear and act anyway, before long the fear itself becomes a trigger to act neurologically. Fear does have its uses, it's there for a reason. When you feel fear and your adrenaline starts pumping and your heart rate increases, it's telling you that you need to get prepared. Get prepared to run. In the context of pursuing your dreams, get prepared to learn, to act and to do whatever it takes.

To start getting into the habit of feeling the fear and acting anyway, put yourself in uncomfortable positions every day, have conversations with people who challenge you, do something adventurous like skydiving, taking on a project you have no idea about, learning something new. The key here is to become obsessed with new experiences that allow you to become accustomed to feeling uncomfortable or fearful and acting anyway. Then the brain can become even better at creating new neural networks, allowing it to become fitter and stronger!

VITAMIN D - DO WHATEVER IT TAKES

A river cuts through rock not because of its power, but its persistence.
— Unknown

An athlete of the mind never quits on their dreams no matter what. Most athletes of the mind have failed more than many and made many more mistakes. Although they take them on board as learnings, not setbacks. An athlete of the mind takes massive action and does whatever it takes, while staying true to his or her values and ethics and remaining within the confines of the law. However, you will find that many will ask for forgiveness rather than permission within the business or financial world.

I believe it's critical to stay sophisticated, honest, and congruent to your values, by doing what feels right to you, whatever that may be at the time. Outside of this there are no excuses, no reasons, no person, and no setback that will ever completely stop an athlete of the mind. In your mind, let there be no failure, only feedback, and the only way for you to fail is to quit. If you never quit you will never fail—simple!

The athlete of the mind is prepared to get up as early as they need to and go to bed as late as they need to achieve their dreams. The athlete of the mind is relentless in the pursuit of their dreams, with such laser beam focus that no obstacle can cause them to take their eye off the prize. People will pass, loved ones will break their hearts, kids will be born, illness will fall upon them, accidents will happen, economies will fail, governments will change power, snow will fall, droughts will occur, floods will come, but they will never, ever, take their eyes off the ultimate prize of their dreams, not even for a second. And if they do, they go straight back there.

In my last business, there was a time that I had to live in my office as I was homeless, but I did not quit. I couldn't afford food and couldn't eat for days on end, but I did not quit. When setting up these current businesses I had glandular fever and was bedridden for months, but I did not quit on my dreams. I worked all day on my laptop and did whatever it took, as I had promises to keep to my loved ones.

No matter what tests or adversity you are faced with, a true athlete of the mind never waivers from their dreams and always keeps at least one eye on the prize.

When you want to succeed as bad as you want to breathe,
then you'll be successful.

— Eric Thomas

VITAMIN E - ELIMINATE NEGATIVE SELF-TALK AND BLAME

I am—two of the most powerful words, for what you put after them shapes your reality.

— Unknown

Quite possibly the quickest and easiest way to get massive changes in the results of our lives is by changing our self-talk. You cannot stop thinking. You think all day, every day, and if you let it, your mind will wander, it will do as it pleases. It will become lazy, distracted and weak if you let it.

The biggest killer of our dreams is not the economy, our parents or the government, not even where we live. The biggest killer of our dreams is the negative self-talk that stops us in our tracks. The negative self-talk that we use to self-sabotage ourselves or our actions. I'm about to share with you the five most powerful forms of negative self-talk through which, if you continue to use them, you will never, ever, ever achieve your dreams. Even if you do, it will be short-lived.

Your brain is a muscle that can be strengthened or weakened. Your mind is also like a garden, and what happens to a garden if we let it go? It grows weeds, right? If we weed our garden once then let it go, what happens? They grow back, right? So, we need to weed the garden of our mind of negative self-talk every day. If we don't the weeds will grow back.

There are many types of weeds in the garden of our mind. In this book, I'm going to cover five of the most devastating weeds that will destroy your garden if you let it. If you choose to begin focusing every day on weeding your garden of the mind of just these five weeds, and do not implement anything else in this book, I'm sure I will be hearing from you very soon about some great success story or something you've achieved in your life due to the positive changes.

WEED 1: THE WORD TRY

Do, or do not, there is no try!

— Yoda – Star Wars.

The word 'try' denotes failure. I 'tried' to quit smoking, I 'tried' to lose weight, I 'tried' to make the relationship work, I 'tried' to eat healthy, and I 'tried' my best to make my dreams a reality.

When you use the word try, it's because you are giving up or stepping back. An athlete of the mind never quits, remember, not on their dreams. The more resistance they experience, the harder they push. Persistence beats resistance. Can you ever remember actually using the word try after you succeeded at something? No, of course not, because you didn't try, you just did it. This is so simple that deep down you probably know that whenever you use the word try, it is holding you back, and causes you to take a step back and stop giving one hundred percent.

Completely remove the word try from your vocabulary. And do not replace it with, 'I gave it my best', or 'I did my best. Did you really? If you gave it your best until you achieved it and did whatever it took then you would have succeeded. Is your best really your best? Could you not do better tomorrow from the learnings? Of course. Eliminate the word try.

WEED 2: THE WORD SHOULD

Have you ever found yourself saying things like, I 'should' go to the gym, I 'should eat healthy', I 'should' save more money, I should, I should, and I should? And you should all over yourself?

When we say we should do something, are we motivated to do it? Not at all. And when we feel we should do something then we don't, how do we feel? Guilty, right? Is guilt a motivational state? Not at all. Then to make it worse, we create an anchor that triggers a feeling of guilt every time we think about what we should do. Let me explain.

Day 1 – 'I should make phone calls' – you don't, then you feel guilty.

Day 2 – 'I should make phone calls' – you don't, then you feel guilty.

Day 3 – 'I should make phone calls' – you don't, then you feel guilty.

Day 4 – You simply think making phone calls and automatically feel guilty and you don't know why.

Have you ever heard a song come on the radio and it's reminded you of someone or an experience? It's called a trigger; you can use these to your advantage or they can be your pitfall.

Instead of using the word should from here on in, you are going to replace it with a strong 'must' and 'because'. Example: I must go to the gym because I want to live longer so I can see my grandkids born.

Start replacing 'should' with 'must' today and watch yourself become a huge action taker. This will also help you eliminate procrastination.

WEED 3: THE WORD LIKE

What a weak word really. I would 'like' to achieve my dream lifestyle. I would 'like' to quit smoking. I would 'like' to be financially free. Do you think the word 'like' is compelling and emotionally pulling enough to motivate you to do whatever it takes to achieve your dreams? Definitely not. Instead of saying 'I would like to', start saying 'I'm going to' today.

WEED 4: THE WORD BUT

The word 'but' is a dream killer. When used in a sentence it negates everything said before it. I would like to go on a date with you 'but', I would like to go to the gym, 'but', I would like to achieve my dreams 'but' I have to put my kids and my family first. I would like to go on a holiday 'but' I can't afford it. I would like to be financially free 'but'.

I understand that when we use it, it seems to make sense to us. But all it does is give you an excuse and a reason not to make it happen. You will also notice when making excuses people use a lot of these words and distinctions together. Kick but in the butt and start moving towards your dreams now. Eliminate all the excuses, use strong compelling words, remember your *why* and tell yourself you are going to do it, no matter what, for your kids, for your family, for your community, and most importantly, for yourself.

WEED 5: BLAME

When you think, everything is someone else's fault you will suffer a lot. When you realize that everything springs only from yourself, you will learn both peace and joy.

— Dalai Lama

This usually follows 'like' and 'but'. 'I would like to eat healthy, but I don't have enough time to prepare my food.' Here we are blaming time and we don't even know it. We are blaming something we cannot control. Therefore, we relinquish all of our power, responsibility and control, meaning we are the victim and powerless to do anything about it. This reality for many is so far from the truth that it's blinding, and I believe that, next to not knowing their *why*, it is the biggest reason people don't succeed in achieving their dreams.

'I would like to spend more time on my business but I need to look after my children.' This is a huge one, and I agree family comes first. But don't use them as an excuse and blame them for you not achieving your dreams. You might think this sounds harsh, and at first it will. If you look deep into your soul I know you will find it to be true. Is it really your kids? Could you not get up earlier? Create more financial freedom and free up your time? Find someone to help out with the kids?

I agree family is the most important thing, which is why you must achieve your hopes and dreams so you can lead by example and show your kids that it is possible and dreams do come true. Imagine the lessons and values they will learn from you when you do.

We usually blame things outside of us, and tie it in with an excuse. 'Sorry I'm late for work, the traffic was bad.' This is so common. If you had left ten minutes earlier would you have been on time? Of course. Can you control the traffic? No. What you can control is what time you leave. So, you are not late because of the traffic, you are late because you didn't leave early enough.

For many this might be hard to grasp at first. When you do, you will start to take full responsibility for everything in your life and become powerful beyond measure, the captain of your own destiny, in charge of directing your path to greatness. You are in control, you are the one.

Blaming usually goes hand in hand with complaining. What's the point in complaining anyway? Does it really get you what you want? If you are honest with yourself does it really, truly make you happy? I challenge you to go just the next seven days without complaining about a thing, and you will begin to notice how happy you feel and how simple life can actually be. If something happens in your life that you cannot control, that is influenced by someone else, say, your boss, there is no point complaining about it to your friends and family, they don't want to hear it. Does that really enrich the quality of your relationship with the person you actually care about? Does it productively solve the problem? Instead of complaining to someone else, try approaching the person directly in an assertive but kind manner, and never say a bad thing about another, as it does you no good, nor does it give you what you desire anyway.

Next time you find yourself making an excuse, complaining, or blaming something or someone outside of you, stop it immediately. If in the future you are late, or something happens, simply say sorry, and don't back it up with an excuse. Take full responsibility for your part in the experience. If someone else does something or it is outside of your control, approach them directly.

Every time you point the finger of blame at someone you have three pointing straight back at you!

— Unknown

4

HOW TO BUILD A 6-FIGURE PERSONAL TRAINING BUSINESS IN 90 DAYS

As you continue to read this book, I understand that the stage you are at with your fitness business will vary from that of others who read this book. Keeping this in mind, I felt it important to ensure I cover all the bases from beginning to end. If you are just starting a fitness business, or are in the eighty percent of trainers making around $1000 a week or less, this is the perfect place to start. If you already have a 6-figure fitness business, I highly recommend reading this chapter nevertheless; this is the largest chapter in the book because it is the foundation chapter. It has more strategies, marketing, sales, systems than any other chapter, because for many, building 6 figures is the hardest part. And I know after personally building over 1200 fitness businesses, that if you can build to 6 figures once, then you can do it again and again and again...

In this chapter, I'm going to pave the exact road for you to follow, the map, the precise steps to building a 6-figure PT business in the next 90 days. You read that right, 90 days! This number will seem un-realistic for many, BUT we have helped hundreds of trainers do this using these systems, in our one-on-one business coaching program, over and over again across the globe. Remember the first step is to believe it's possible. If you don't believe it's possible then I can't help you!

In this chapter, we will lay the heavy base, a strong foundation to build upon. And like a high-rise building, the stronger your foun-dation, the larger the business you can build upon it. I understand not everyone wants a 7-figure business or a massive company, and I get that. I also understand the primary goal for many is not money, which is also why I have broken this book down into building to **6 figures in 90 days, $250,000 a year in 6 Months, and 7 figures in 12 months,** and shared with you the exact steps along the way.

There are three main business steps to building a 7-figure fitness business:

1. Book yourself solid (gives you 6 figures in 3-6 months) THIS CHAPTER!
2. Create leverage and passive income (gives you $250,000 a year in 6-12 months)
3. Create financial and time freedom (gives you a 7-figure+ fitness business in 12-24 months).

You cannot take step three without taking the second step, and you cannot take the second step without taking the first step. It's not possible. Many business owners want to spend all this time ON their business and I can understand that. But in the beginning, you need to get your hands dirty, do the hard work, and get in the trenches, as this will be the fastest way to get you to your goal of 7 figures without borrowing a ton of money or taking a ridiculous amount of time. It sucks digging through all the dirt to find the gold. But as you find more gold it will get easier to find more gold. (Gold being clients). This chapter focuses on the first step of the above three steps, and that is to book yourself solid first, to lay the strong foundation with sales, marketing and systems before we create leverage, and then freedom!

So, let's take the first step together, here we go…

AWARENESS

If you are reading this book, then I'm guessing you want more. More income, more leads, more freedom, more clients, more balance or even more leverage. If you wish to have more of something, this means you wish and need to change something.

The first focal point in any change is awareness—awareness of where you are first, then where you wish to be, then how to get there, in that order.

Firstly, it is important to be aware of WHY you want to generate the $100,000+ a year. It's not for the pieces of paper or plastic, it will be for a reason; what is your driving force? Is it for family, to buy a home, car, charity, travel etcetera.? What is the emotional pull?

Take a moment now to write down on a piece of paper why you want to make $100,000 plus a year, then make it even more compelling. If you haven't done that yet, then just take a moment in your mind's eye to think about *why* right now. *Why* do you REALLY want this? And as you think about that reason, simply ask yourself, '*Why* is that so important to me'?

The person who becomes the most successful is not the most skilled, the most intelligent, the best at what they do—they are the hungriest. And hunger comes from WHY you want this and what it will mean for you!

Once you have in your mind the reason *why* it is so important, ask yourself, 'What does that really mean for me?' Or even better, take a moment now to write down your answers to these questions.

Why is it so important I build a 6-figure Business?

_____

_____

_____

_____

_____

What would that really mean for me?

_____

_____

_____

_____

_____

Now we have our motivation and our driving force we can work out where we want to be and by when. But first take a moment to answer these questions, to really pin point exactly why this is so important for you…

How would I feel if in 6–12 months if I'm still exactly where I am now?

_____

_____

_____

_____

_____

BUT How would I feel if in 6–12 months if I take massive action and follow the steps in this book, and I do build a 6- then 7-figure fitness business?

_____

_____

_____

_____

_____

If I Keep doing what I have been doing up until now, am I guaranteed to achieve this goal?

YES/NO

So, you need to make some changes, right? What changes are you prepared to make to make this a reality?

_____

_____

_____

_____

_____

YOUR GOALS AND ACTION PLAN

The purpose of this section is to determine exactly when you want to reach 6 figures and what you need to do to reach it. For example, if you charge $50 for 30-minute PT sessions you need 40 PT sessions a week to hit 6 figures ($2000 a week).

By not setting goals in your life you leave life to chance and never really achieve your full potential. Just as having a deadline helps to more effectively achieve a task, having goals can give us something to focus on, then create a plan and act towards the attainment of it. By knowing what we want in life with specificity, we create clarity and certainty. Then we can reverse engineer the desired outcome by playing the numbers game (not the emotional roller coaster game) and determine precise strategies for achieving it. We then monitor our progress and guarantee results by flexibly applying the strategies and systems.

Does this mean we always achieve every goal? Of course not; what we do always achieve is an outcome, whether the outcome we wish for or not. By setting goals we can choose the outcomes we wish to experience and work towards them. Otherwise we just live life and hope for the best. We react to our business, rather than designing our business.

They say five percent of the world's population effectively set goals, and approximately the other ninety-five percent work for that five percent. It is also documented that just one percent of people on this earth earn ninety-five percent of the world's income; and guess what they ALL have in common? That's right, they set goals. Of course, this doesn't mean everyone wants to earn millions, it just means we understand we can achieve more, be more, do more and give more with this clarity.

It is important to remember that it's not just about achieving the goal, It's about what we learn on the journey, and the person it helps us become. It is also important to note that we have business goals for the purpose of achieving our personal goals, and we have personal goals because they are the things that lead to ultimate happiness and fulfillment in life. Whether it's to make millions, achieve a sporting triumph, or spend more quality time with family.

By planning these things and having goals, it will make these things seem more realistic, giving you more clarity and a sense of certainty and confidence. That confidence causes you to take more action and build greater momentum. So be as specific as possible, and think about it as a to do list; include financial, health, relationships, achievements, and think of it as a catalogue of the universe, to select from what you choose at will, even if you don't feel you know how to achieve it yet.

Simply write all the things you wish to achieve and/or do each month for the next six months and remember to be as SPECIFIC as you can and include your ultimate sessions.

E.g. if it is January, by June I, wish to have 40 booked sessions; then chunk it down – January have 10, February have 15, March have 25, April have 30, May have 35 and June have 40.

TIP:
Remember to include the following...

- Bank accounts: You will need a business bank account, register your business if you haven't yet, ABN, Personal Bank account to pay yourself into, GST offset account to put tax aside into, and a savings account
- Team members: accountant, bookkeeper, solicitor, business coach, mentor
- Income projections and goals
- Total clients
- Total sessions
- Marketing stuff
- Venues and equipment
- Branding, websites, logo
- Personal goals: relationships, health and finances
- Advertising and sales
- Articles, video profiles, Facebook group etc.
- Database and social media

SET YOUR TARGETS AND KEY PERFORMANCE INDICATORS (KPIS)

Probably the most important part of this chapter is your marketing funnel for determining your targets then implementing strategies to achieve them. This is the fundamental principal we use in the

Quantum Fitness Marketing Program to guarantee results. If you choose to stick to this process you will be very successful and build to 6 figures incredibly fast.

Picture this: if you were to charge a client just $99 a week for 2 x 30-minute PT sessions and picked up just 2 clients a week, after 2 years you would be earning $1,000,000—a million dollars a year, 1 MILLION. Now I'm sure you will agree that if you had the right guidance and support with the 'how to' marketing strategies that is very possible... (We will discuss this later in this book).

This process is very simple, but if you skip it and don't use this on a weekly basis, you WILL NOT build a 6-figure business, let alone a 7-figure business. And if you are perhaps lucky enough to reach that goal, you probably won't keep it!

Part 1: Determine how many PT clients and sessions you want in total for yourself to deliver personally (as you can take staff through the same process later). Example: if you are doing 30-minute PT sessions and want to do 20 hours a week, your goal would be 40 sessions and 20 clients doing 2 sessions each.

Part 2: Once you have these figures, choose an exact date and write that exact date into your action plan. For the sake of the process, let's say you are currently doing just 10 sessions each week and your goal is to do 50 sessions total yourself. Today's date is Monday 8th January and I want 50 sessions by Monday 26 March (12 weeks).

Part 3: We then reverse engineer it from there to determine how many sessions each week we need to pick up to ensure we reach our target (the same process we use with clients who want to lose weight), which works out to just over 3 x new PT sessions each week or 2 clients. (Remember to put this in your action plan).

Part 4: Then the question is this: how many free consults do you need to do (who 'showed') to guarantee you pick up 2 x clients each week based roughly on your current conversion rate? You might say well, my conversion rate is around 50% or about 2 out of every 4 showed consults. So, if I do 4 showed consults each week then that will give me my 2 clients. Then as we know people cancel, how many BOOKED consults do we need to book to ensure we have 4 showed? You might say well 8 booked with 4 cancelled will guarantee me a minimum of 2 clients each week.

Part 5: Lastly, the question to ask yourself (don't worry about the how-to yet) is, how many leads or enquiries do you need to generate to guarantee you can book in 8 complimentary sessions? At this point I like to over-compensate and underestimate, so if you are saying 20, I'm going to recommend 30 leads a week to GUARANTEE you will book 8.

It will look like this:
Generate 30 x Leads
Book 8 comp sessions
Show 4 comp sessions
Secure 2 new clients/2 x PT sessions = 4 sessions week

HOWEVER: As above, I like to over-compensate and underestimate, so here are the numbers I recommend all clients.

Generate 30 x Leads
Book 14 comp sessions
Show 8 comp sessions
Secure 2 new clients/2 x PT sessions = 4 sessions week

If you play the above numbers game you will definitely see how 6 figures in 90 days is very possible. This is why so many personal trainers using our systems all across the globe are crushing it, because they are playing these numbers. I understand you may be thinking, that's great Jason, but how the heck do I get 30-50 leads every week?

Well that's exactly what I will show you in this book if you keep reading!

IF YOU WISH TO BUILD 7 FIGURES IN 12 MONTHS, HERE ARE THE TARGETS:

Generate 50 leads week

Book 14 consults

Show 8 consults

Gain 4 new clients/8 new sessions week

This will then be placed somewhere you can see every day, perhaps in your diary, and will form the focus of your dedication to achieving your goal of 6 figures; for this example would give you 50 sessions x $50 = $2500 a week, or even 50 sessions x $40 = $2000 a week, and $100,000 a year.

NOTE: Your number 1 focus is to generate 30 leads+ a week; I will show you how to do this later in this book.

SIDE NOTE: remember your minimums don't have to be your maximums.

SALES SYSTEMS

CREATE YOUR FREE CONSULT PROCESS

Now we have your action plan and marketing funnel targets in place. Before we start to generate leads, we need to make sure we are not wasting our leads. We do this by refining our sales system so that it is effective. It's important to maximize your profit margins and your conversion rates before beginning to sell your personal training service. In this section, you will not only find a template for a complete one hour sales process to increase your sales, but also example templates for a pre-exercise questionnaire, terms and conditions, referral slip, vouchers, package power points, and more.

If you use the information below to create and refine your process, you will exponentially increase your sales.

I am even going to share with you the packages we use in our own business. Remember to determine your packages and business model it is important to know your intention; also, the size of your business plays a huge role. There is more than one business model or system that may work for you; below is simply a guide to make it easy for you to get organized.

TAKING CASH VS DIRECT DEBIT

Every time you take cash from a client it sets a negative anchor of pain (loss of money) then triggers every time that whenever your client meets you they associate you with them giving you money.

If you are relying on your clients to show to the session then hand you the money, or even transfer the money, who has control over your income? You or your clients? Your clients, right?

But imagine if you had direct debit set up so every week you get all the payments in one lump sum, and you can literally adjust payments online. Who has control of your income, you or your clients? You do, right?

Who would you rather have control over your income? You or your clients?

Direct debit is free for Personal Trainers; and besides, how many people check their account regularly?

Cash looks unprofessional. As a rule of thumb, never be seen taking cash on the gym floor. Have your client place it in an envelope if necessary.

Direct debit is easy, and the company sends you all the reports so you don't have to do them yourself, plus follows up on missed payments. (Much more organized).

When taking cash, you will minimize your income for 2 reasons: 1. When you have cash on you, you are more likely to spend it. 2.

When someone cancels, and they will when they owe you money, you cannot charge them for the session.

Direct debit means your clients pay ahead, so if they cancel within the 24-hour cancellation policy, you can still charge them.

So you see, direct debit gives you more control and more income, while making it easier to operate your business.

PACKAGES

As a coach to Personal Trainers all over the world, one of the biggest questions I am asked is, should I sell personal training in package form?

Well, after helping thousand of PTs worldwide build their business in some shape or form, and selling tens of thousands of PT sessions personally, it seems it is indeed a far more lucrative and effective strategy to sell in package form. Let me explain the two main essential reasons why.

1. Perceived increased value:

In package form, there is a plethora of extras you can add to the package at no extra cost to you, making the package seem even more extensive and even more valuable than selling individual sessions. ALL one-on-one PT sessions are thirty minutes, as it is more time efficient and enables you to increase your earning potential.

2. You can charge more for each session:

If at the gym someone asks you 'how much do you charge per session?' Then you say '$50 per 30 minutes' you may lose that prospect there and then. Alternatively, you want to suggest, 'I have different packages available depending on a person's needs; so what we will do is schedule you in for a free one hour complimentary session so I can establish a deeper understanding of the goals you want to achieve, and then I can more clearly educate you on the best package available'. Then continue to book them in and upsell PT in the comp session.

By selling results rather than time, it increases the perceived value.

Here are the three packages we personally used:

1. The Full Monty package – for females wanting to tone
2. The Easy Weight loss package – A unisex package for people wanting to lose 10kg plus
3. The Power Source package – A package for guys wanting strength, size, or focus on weight training.

All packages are power point presentations, which will have your personal name on, and be kept on your laptop desktop for easy access.

COMPLIMENTARY SESSION PROCESS

The fastest way to get in front of more people is to offer some kind of try-before-you-buy. Before buying a car, I want to test drive it. Before buying a home I want to walk through it. Before paying a PT I want to experience them first.

To be a successful Personal Trainer and successfully grow our client base, it is important to have a well-structured free consultation process to help educate people on the importance of why they need a Personal Trainer to achieve their results. If the number one intention of a complimentary session is to pick the person up as a client and help them achieve their results faster and more effectively, then it makes sense that all the tools we use in this process are conducive to helping us achieve this result.

The tools required and supplied are as follows:

- Pre-exercise questionnaire
- Power point presentation of package
- Terms and conditions of appropriate package
- Direct debit Forms

- Business cards
- Diary, pen and highlighters
- Gift vouchers
- Meet and greet

You will meet your potential client on time at reception. Introduce yourself by saying: 'Hi <NAME> I'm Jason. your Personal Trainer. It's a pleasure to meet you. Let's take a seat over here' (gesture towards seat with an open hand). If they have a bag, direct them to a locker. Ask them how their day has been, and be sure to have your pre-exercise questionnaire form ready with their basic details already filled in. Then say, 'I'll just get you to take a seat and fill this out, and I'll come straight back.'

Once they have filled in the form, continue by sitting down NEXT to them in an open posture. Example: if you are right handed you will sit on their right so they can see you writing.

PRE-EXERCISE QUESTIONNAIRE

There are three main reasons why we use a pre-exercise questionnaire. Some of you may say, 'well Jason, surely we need to learn about the history of the client and about any injuries'. Yes, this is true. Plus we need to learn about their lifestyle and personal information to assist them more effectively, and we also need to learn about their goals, and what they wish to achieve so we can determine the best path of action to take.

These are the main, but not all the vital elements to an effective pre-ex; but which is the most important? The number one intention of having a pre-ex is to gather as much information about the person as possible so you can effectively communicate why they need you as a PT, and to help them achieve their results. We understand that, as trainers, the fastest and best way to help people achieve their goals is by seeing them through to their goals—is it not?

If the above statements are true, then it would seem the intelligent thing to do is structure the pre-ex in a way that will achieve that outcome; to pick them up as a client and personally guide them to their goal by keeping them accountable. Some of you may be thinking, 'well that's great Jason, but injuries and past history are important also'. Yes, they are, but they are there for us to learn more about the client and for insurance purposes.

OK; so what is the most effective way to structure a pre-ex? After personally delivering over 3000 comp sessions, free consultations, inductions, or whatever you would like to call them, I have found the following structure to be the most effective; it has three main parts:

The following three parts may seem standard to you, but it's the underlying detail and slight nuances that make the difference in your success.

Part 1: Personal details:
These include the logical facts: name, address, DOB, workplace, phone and email. Most people skim through this part, but this is the most important part, and should take about ten minutes to go through. It is absolutely vital to build rapport by learning about the individual on a personal level. Thus you can form a bond, a connection, so they understand they can trust you and your genuinely wish to help them.

I love this part, because imagine how much you can learn about a person if you ask open-ended questions. Example: I see you live close by, which will make it easy for you to get here. How long have you been living there? Who do you live with? Do you have children, husband, partner etcetera? What are their names? How long have you been there? Where were you before that? If you could live anywhere, where would you live?

You have written here that you are a plumber; how long have you been doing it for? What did you do before that? How do you enjoy it? Is it good money? Oh, it's your birthday soon, are you doing much?

Are you drinking or not/partying? If you could do anything, what would you do? Cute email address... etcetera...

From these questions and information, you can learn about the person's values, beliefs, income, family, lifestyle, habits, and hobbies. Do you think this information will be extremely useful? Remember this is the part they get to talk about themselves and you listen and connect.

Part 2: Results:

This part should take around fifteen minutes and include information from the 4 Ws—What/Where/When/Why/How.

So <NAME>, tell me about the results you want to achieve. (Always ask rather than read from the sheet, so they can associate with the feelings they draw from talking about it, and feel the sensations more powerfully). What do you want to achieve? Fitness, weight loss, strength, muscle gain etcetera... Example: I notice you've said you would like to lose weight. Tell me about that.

Where do you want to achieve it? Arms, legs, stomach, thighs, chest, shoulders waist, hips etcetera... You wish to lose weight, and you've said here you would like to focus on your butt and thighs. (This is a great opportunity to ask about clothing size, and last time they were happy).

When do you want to achieve it by? 1month, 3, and 6 etcetera... Example: 6 months...

Why do you want to achieve it by then? Example: I am getting married.

The 4 Ws give us specific information so that when we deliver our first session, we can focus on their specific results, so they know we are listening and are really going to fast track their results. Some more questions:

How would you feel in 6 months if you haven't achieved your results?

Then how would you feel in 6 months if you have achieved your results?

Finally, you want to reiterate the importance of them achieving their goals by asking, on a scale of 1-10, how important is it? This really helps the person realize consciously just how important these results are. Be sure to ask, because if they wrote 8 on the form and you have done this right, they will now give it a 10. If they still just say 8 or 9, simply respond by saying, just a 9? They will usually increase it themselves.

Then ask, why it is so important to you? Once they answer, ask them, and what does that really mean for you? Take your time to have the person explain their results in their own words, and again, *listen*.

Part 3 Personal history and injuries:
This part should only take about 5 minutes, which means the whole process is about 30 minutes, then a 20-minute workout specific to their results, and a 10-minute close; include heart problems, smoking, pregnancy, epilepsy, blood pressure etcetera...

If you are ever unsure, refer the person to a doctor to attain a medical certificate before training them. Finally, at the very bottom, it is important to have a waiver stating you are not a medical professional, and this is just a guide for exercise; then get it signed and dated.

Some of you may be asking, 'well Jason what about blood pressure, skin folds, weight' etcetera... Personally, when doing fitness testing, I don't do it on the initial consultation. You can use/log a separate piece of paper for that. Remember, the intention is to build rapport and pick up the person as a client. The last thing you want to do is intimidate the person the first time you meet them. Get to know them build rapport first.

Once you have covered all the above items, simply ask if they have any questions before we do a workout, and give them a brief description of what you will be doing today.

THE WORKOUT

It is important to remember that if you are taking someone through a free comp session, there is a good chance they haven't exercised for some time, maybe even ever, and it is important we leave them feeling good, as it is a feel-good session. At the same time you want them to realize how unfit they actually are.

Remember to do an effective warm-up, keeping in mind the session will only go for about 20 minutes in total.

Even during the workout, your potential client is judging you to determine if you are genuine, if you are the right trainer for them, and even if they want or need PT. So it is important to focus your first workout with them around the fact you are still selling to them.

This is why, after delivering 3000 comp sessions myself, I recommend doing a full body blast, which usually focuses on 80% lower body and 20% upper body for females, and 80% upper body and 20% lower body for males, using compound and functional movements and focusing on the following two things:

1) Use exercises they cannot do on their own. If they feel as though they can do it on their own, they will not see a need to have you there, so train a little heavier, and use hands-on spotting; do partnered work including med ball, boxing and kicking.

2) Focus on the results they want and the areas they want. If their number one priority is their thighs, then leg presses, squats, lunges, step-ups are going to be an effective way to have them feel their workout for several days, and they will feel like you listened. Remember to do a small cool down, but we still want their heart rate elevated and the endorphins running when we present the package options. So there won't be much time to stretch; if you feel it's necessary, have them do a light cool down and stretch on their own once completed.

THE PRESENTATION

Then continue with your three YES sets.

1) So <NAME>, did you enjoy the workout? 2) Can you see how by doing this on a regular basis you will fast track your results? 3) Can you see yourself training like this on a regular basis?

During this time, you want to prepare your laptop, and have it open and ready to present the necessary power point presentation. Then say, 'based on what we have gone through today, and the fact that you have said...' (relay 3 things back to them they specifically said themselves: e.g. 'you want to lose 20 kgs and you have given it a 10 out of 10, plus it is really important to you because...') 'I believe you need to Invest in <name of the package>'.

Play the power point presentation and read through the solution. All the packages include items that add increased value to each item; explain why it is so important for them, then ask 'How does this look to you <name>'? If they say good, respond with, just good?

'So, with this package you have two options. The first option is the weekly option, which is simply weekly installments of just $149 each week for everything in the package. Or <name>, you have the fortnightly option, which is fortnightly installments of $298; they work out exactly the same. We understand that most people get paid either weekly or fortnightly. So <name>, do you get paid weekly or fortnightly?' PAUSE... and wait for their response.

Example: if they say weekly, respond with, 'so weekly will be easier for you?' Once they say yes, again say, 'OK then, we will get you started on the weekly option, yes.'

OPTIONAL: If they comment on the <Pay upfront and save section> or you choose to offer them the upfront option, still complete the above and simply say the following:

'We also have an upfront option, where you can save a substantial amount of money. So for the Full Monty 50 pack it would only be $1999, and you would save $451 which is a huge saving. How do you feel about doing it that way?'

Please note: If they are paying in advance they will still fill out two terms and conditions and a direct debit form; the DD form will be for one payment only, the total amount.

DROP SELLS

We always sell at three sessions, so If they say they cannot afford it, reply, 'besides money, is there anything stopping, you from getting started right now?' They will usually say no. Then say OK, what If I were to make it easier for you by making it just $99 each week, and you will still see me twice a week, and receive everything in the package to guarantee your results, would that be easier for you?

If they still say they cannot afford it, say 'Ok then, what if I make it even easier for you by making it as little as $49 a week for everything in the package; you will still see me once a week and that way we can keep you on track and accountable for achieving your goals? Would that be easier for you?'

If they still say they cannot afford it say, 'Ok well we do have a special offer at the moment, which is called the Kick Start Pack, and this will give you three more 30-minute Personal Training sessions after today for only $99; it's a one time offer only. How do you feel about doing that?' Wait for a response, then continue...

This allows you to get two to three no's before you get your yes, drastically increasing your conversion rate.

Once they say yes, prepare two terms and conditions for the appropriate package, and go through completing them; one copy is for the client and one copy is for the business. Then have them fill out the direct debit form with a signature. If they don't know their details, simply have them sign it and have them text you when they are home; OR ask which bank they are with and call their bank there and then on your mobile for their details. If it is completed in its entirety, the pink slip is given to the client. It is important to remember that all clients pay in advance, so if their first paid session is next week, ideally their first payment is this week, preferably making all debits Thursdays or Fridays.

Remember, if you have time and they don't know their details, simply pull out your mobile phone and call their bank.

The new client is then scheduled for their follow-up and given your business card with their next appointment date written on the back.

You will then give the client a gift voucher for two free PT sessions for a friend or family member, and the referral slip to enter two friends or family members into the draw to win one-month free PT. Then take the pre-ex, terms and conditions and direct debit form, and file them safely.

TO SEE THE VIDEO Version of the entire sales process, simply visit this link → https://youtu.be/0dpU9fWs254

ALSO, I have pre-recorded a video on the psychology of sales, which you can watch here → https://youtu.be/32UM4sNwam4

IMPORTANT: See the following pages for template examples.
- Pre-exercise questionnaire
- Terms and conditions
- PowerPoint package template
- Referral slip
- 2 Free PT Session gift voucher

Pre-Exercise Questionnaire

Name _____   DOB _____

Address _____ Email_____

Phone work _____ Home_____ Mobile_____

Occupation _____

What results do you wish to achieve?

☐ Reduce body fat   ☐ Strength training   ☐ Weight Loss
☐ Stress management   ☐ Reshaping   ☐ Increase fitness
☐ Sports conditioning ☐ Improve muscle tone   ☐ Improve flexibility
☐ Rehabilitation   ☐ Tone   ☐ Other _____

Where do you want to achieve your results?

☐ Thighs   ☐ Back   ☐ Lower back
☐ Stomach   ☐ Arms   ☐ Hips
☐ Buttocks   ☐ Arms   ☐ Waist
☐ Chest   ☐ Calves   ☐ Other _____

When would you like to achieve these results? _____

Why would you like to achieve these results then?_____

How many days a week do you wish to exercise?_____

How long have you been thinking about it?_____

What has kept you from starting sooner?_____

On a scale from 1–10 how important is it for you to achieve your results?
1 2 3 4 5 6 7 8 9 10

Why is it so important for you to achieve these results? _____

Do you smoke?   Yes   No

Are you pregnant?   Yes   No

Have you ever had or experienced?

☐ Heart trouble/history ☐ Arthritis ☐ Epilepsy

☐ Pain in the chest ☐ Asthma ☐ Sports injury

☐ Faint or dizzy spells ☐ Bone or joint problems ☐ Depression

☐ High blood pressure ☐ Back problems ☐ Other _____

I understand that my personal trainer is not able to provide me with medical advice with regard to any medical conditions I may have and that this information is used only as a guideline to the limitations of my ability to exercise. I will not hold my personal trainer liable in any way for any injuries that may occur while I am training.

Signed_____ Date_____ Your PT _____

Terms and Conditions

Options:

☐ Weekly installments   ☐ Fortnightly installments   ☐ Single Payment

Of amount $_____

I _____ agree to these terms and understand the following:

This_____ package entitles the signatory to_____ personal training sessions each week/total plus a free 30 minute follow up session, monthly updated program, nutritional advice, reassessment each month, 2 free personal training sessions for 2 friends, monthly newsletter and regular information via Facebook, regular social events and 100% money back guarantee if you stick to everything we plan for you and still don't get your results.

This agreement is for a minimum of _____ weeks being the date of _____ or is only valid until _____.

Any sessions not used by the expiry date above will be forfeited and in no way are any refunds given. If sessions are not completed within the minimum term amounts will still be debited as per this agreement until the end of the minimum term; if you wish payments to stop you can email the address below, otherwise they will continue. However, you can suspend your payments at any time for a minimum of 4 weeks only. 24 hour's notice is required for cancellations or the session may be forfeited.

This package is non-refundable and not valid with any other offer. If you are late to a session, it will still finish 30minutes after the agreed start time. For all account enquiries simply email **<your email address>**

Note: No more than 1 month of personal training can be paid for in advance and single payments only can be paid through EFT and transferred before the second session (follow up).

Time to fast track your results...

Signed_____ Date_____ Your PT_____

Committed to your results!

Easy Weight Loss Package

PRESENTED BY YOUR PT EXPERT™ *JASON GROSSMAN.*

The Solution

Do you want to burn more fat while you sleep?

Then this package will reveal all the vital 'how to' secrets necessary for shedding those extra unwanted kilos.

I will take you through a specific step by step plan, monitoring your success and motivating your every step to ensure you will achieve your desired results and maximum weight loss.

The Package Includes

- 3 x 30 minute one on one Results Training sessions each week focusing on all aspects including cardio, resistance training, boxing, kick pads, medicine balls and more
- 1 x FREE 30 minute one on one Results Training sessions
- Personal Training diary to promote laser beam focus
- Personal Program updated monthly
- Nutritional guidance
- Goal setting and re-assessment every 4 weeks
- 2 x FREE Personal Training sessions for a friend or family member
- Regular educational information via email, Facebook and Website
- Social events
- 100% money back guarantee

Your Options

All options are direct debit

Weekly	Fortnightly
147	294

Congratulations

"Congratulations on making the life enhancing decision to lose weight, feel great and achieve the results you truly deserve."

Jason Grossman.

Referal Slip

$199 Personal Training Prize Draw

Congratulations you have successfully entered

Name: _____

Mobile: _____

And

Name: _____

Mobile: _____

Into the prize draw to win 1 Month FREE Personal Training Sessions valued at $199

Conditions Apply...   Your PT: _____

OVERCOMING OBJECTIONS

Besides money, time, I'll think about it, I'll talk to my partner are big objections. Here is how you can begin to become a word wizard and overcome any objection.

Step 1) **Empathize and Isolate:** Besides that, is there anything else stopping you from getting started now?

Step 2) **Specify:** (chunk down)

Step 3) **Neutralize:**

Step 4) **Ask closing question again:** Do you have any more questions, or are you ready to get started?

What's the one thing stopping you from getting started right now?

What's the one question you need to ask me; what information do you need to be ready to get started right now?

Besides \<that>, is there anything stopping you from getting started right now?

I WANT TO THINK ABOUT IT:

1. What exactly would you like to think about?
2. What would need to happen right now for you to say yes and start getting your results?
3. What's the one question that you need to ask me right now that will give you enough information to get started?

TALK TO MY PARTNER:

1. What exactly do you need to talk to your partner about?
2. If your partner were here right now, do you think he/she would be supportive? If he/she were here right now, what would they say?
3. Has there ever been a time that your partner has bought something when you weren't there that you were supportive of?
4. Have you ever bought something for yourself without your partner there?

CHECK MY BUDGET:

1. Which part of your budget do you need to check?
2. If you where to find the $99 a week in your budget right now, where would you find it?
3. What actions would you need to take to be able to afford it?
4. If you stopped spending $99 on a week right now, what is one thing in your budget that would allow you to achieve your results faster AND be able to afford this program to guarantee your results?

MORE INFO:

1. What exactly would you like more info on?
2. What's the one question you need to ask me which will give you the answer you need to get started?

I'M NOT SURE IF I NEED IT OR IF IT'S FOR ME:

1. What would need to happen for you to feel like it is for you?
2. How would you know it is for you, and what would you need to happen then...?
3. Sometimes we don't know if something is or is not for us until we just give it a go and get started. Then once we start, we realize how important it is. Have you experienced that before?

MARKETING

Now we have your action plan and targets with what you want, we need to determine the 'how to get you there'. The road map for the journey. The recipe for success!

Now we can begin to market your service (which we will refine shortly). Just like any area of business, by having a plan we can increase your success rate, so below you will find a list of marketing strategies you can use along with an example spreadsheet to create and add to the file with your action plan. Simply place all strategies evenly in a spreadsheet and follow weekly.

The key with marketing is to stack multiple strategies to hedge against failure. Below I have included my top five favourite internal strategies and top five external strategies, PLUS the number one strategy, with details for each rental PT, Mobile PT and studio owner.

As I write this, we have over 50 offline marketing strategies and 100 online strategies. Obviously, I cannot squeeze them all into this book so here are some of my favourite and most powerful ones.

INTERNAL:

1) Referral campaign
2) Bring a friend free week
3) Social events, including workshops and info evenings/seminars
4) Client appreciation day
5) Newsletter monthly via email.

EXTERNAL:

1) Lead boxes and allied health professionals
2) Social media – Facebook group and advertising
3) Business directories online
4) Website with SEO
5) Prize draws

NUMBER 1 STRATEGY AS A RENTAL TRAINER: FLOOR WALKING COMPETITION

I remember nearly eighteen years ago starting as a PT for the first time. In the health club I was working in, new members weren't automatically booked in for a free consultation, so we actually had to sell initial consultations off the floor for $60, and then in those consultations sell PT packages valued at $1000, $3000 and $5000, and the $1000 package didn't even have a payment plan.

Today it seems health clubs and fitness professionals are more sales savvy and understand the importance of 'try before you buy' to maximize conversion rates.

Even with having to sell inductions off the floor, I still managed to book myself solid in less than 12 weeks. After trialing many approaches and experimenting with a plethora of strategies, I came to realize that like most things, there is a science to picking up clients from the floor.

Some of you may say, 'well Jason, that may be over analyzing it a little'; but wouldn't you agree that by having a plan in most areas of your business, with a tracking and follow up system, you will guarantee results, or at least exponentially improve them?

You may already be doing some floor walking, but could you be doing it more effectively? Do you have a plan, or do you wing it?

If I could share with you some very simple strategies to take the awkwardness out of floor walking, make it less salesy, whilst creating a steady flow of leads and clients for you, would that cause you to keep reading?

If you are still reading this, then I'm guessing you are paying rent at a gym or Health Club and may even just be starting out. The biggest mistake many trainers make in your position is they think that the gym or health club is going to do all the work for them. Errr-rrtttt—WRONG... If you are serious about results, then the following things are absolutely vital to your success.

Spend as much time there as possible, even if it is simply working out, studying, or making phone calls. Determine how many hours' worth of sessions you wish to do ultimately and the times of day, and condition yourself to be there right from the start to fill those time slots. If you do rostered hours and then go home, your success will be very limited. Your rostered hours are just the beginning. I originally spent seven days a week, open to close, at the club to reach a 6 figure income in my first 6 months ever as a PT.

Make as many phone calls as possible. Most health clubs or gyms can print out a no show report which has a list of members who haven't been to the gym for some time. You can give them a ring and offer them a free session to help get them kick started again. Talk to and build rapport with the manager, PTM and membership consultants; ask them on a regular basis if they have anyone they need to be rung for a free consult or motivation. Remember to have a spreadsheet to add all your prospects to. If there is a community diary at reception, go through the previous month of cancellations and no shows to ring them and reschedule an appointment.

Talk to ALL members and remember their name. I have a rule for all our trainers that upon passing a member for the third time without speaking to them, stop and introduce yourself, learn their name and remember it. Imagine if you knew every member's name when they are after results or PT; who do you think they will ask? Think of the busiest PT in the gym and now think of the PT in the gym that knows more members by their first name. I'm guessing they are the same trainer.

So floor walking is just about going, OK, I have thirty minutes to talk to as many members on the floor as possible. It is an ongoing process. By talking to members regularly, you will build more rapport, more relationships and have more clients.

If you wish to be very successful at picking up clients in the gym here is a simple formula:

1. Determine how many new clients you wish to gain from this process each week; example: 2.

2. Then determine based on your current conversion rate how many showed comps you need to complete to pick up 2 clients; example: 50% conversion so 4 comps.

3. Take into consideration cancellations for comps and add the extra; example: 6 total comps booked which is just over 1 each day.

4. So, our goal is to book 1 person in off the floor each day. Knowing your strengths and weaknesses, how many people will you need to talk to to book 1 person each day. A good example here is to offer 3 people each day a comp session.

5. Lastly, not everyone you speak to will give you the opportunity to offer a free comp session, or the timing might not be appropriate. Add that to your tally and you might have 4 people each day to speak to. It's that easy.

So your goal would simply be to talk to just 4 people each day, to offer 3 people a free comp session, to book one in, giving you 6 booked and roughly 4 showed prospects at a 50% conversion rate, which is 2 new clients each week. If you did this every week for 6 months you would be earning over $100,000 each year. Sound simple enough?

Now you have a guide and targets to work with, and I'm sure you will agree the above process is simple enough for you to follow with consistency.

OK, we have our targets, but how do we approach people on the floor effectively?

Step 1) Break through the wall (build rapport):
I personally prefer to talk to people on the cardio section, as you will normally have longer to speak to the person. Have you ever approached someone in the gym and they have that look on their face like 'What do you want?' That is the wall I'm talking about? The key to breaking through the wall with a sledgehammer is to show interest in the person first and build rapport.

Example: you approach someone and say Hi, my name is Jason. I've seen you in here a few times but we haven't had the opportunity to speak yet. They will usually respond with their name, to which you may reply, so how was your day? Continue to ask open-ended questions—so what do you do for work? Do you live nearby? Ask personal questions only, not related to exercise; continue this process until the wall disappears. This may take sixty seconds to five minutes. You will know when the wall is gone, as you have experienced it many times before.

Step 2) Build a bridge (determine their fitness goals):
Once the wall is gone we can then build a bridge to us by asking, so how is your training going? Now we all know what people say then, right? It's OK, could be better (this is what we want). What exactly are you wanting to achieve? They might want to lose 10 kg etcetera. Find out how they are eating, what training they are doing etcetera. And very important: and that isn't happening for you at the moment? OR So things aren't going as planned yet? Once they say no, you have built the bridge.

Step 3) Cross the bridge (schedule their comp session):
As soon as they say no, you then say well, what if I were to offer you a free one hour consultation to help get you kick started and fast track your results? I mean if we were to do that, would morning or afternoon be easier for you? Wait for them to answer, then schedule them in and write the appointment time on one of your cards and give it to them.

Occasionally people may say no, but it is a numbers game. If the above process isn't working for you, simply increase the number of people you approach. Even if they say no, once they begin to see how busy you are, they will be chasing you to train. Oh yeah, never chase too hard, as you will end up on a wild goose chase. Here you have a very specific step-by-step process for generating a 6-figure income from one simple strategy. I guarantee personally that if you do this for 6 months, you will be earning 6 figures. I have seen it personally dozens of times.

FLOOR WALKING SCRIPT

Hi, my name, is Jason and I am a Personal Trainer here. Just wondering how would you feel if I were to give you the chance to win one-month free personal training valued at $196?

If yes, write them on the clipboard sheet found on the next page. Keep going until you have 5 each day/30 total. Then announce a winner.

PHONE SCRIPT TO SCHEDULE FLOOR LEADS

Once you have drawn a winner, the next step is to ring the remaining 29+ people and book them in for a free consult using the phone script below.

Hi <NAME>, this is Jason, your Personal Trainer from (NAME OF GYM). I am calling because this week you entered the prize draw to win one month free PT sessions valued at $200... pause... unfortunately you didn't win that prize, however I would like to offer you a free one hour one-on-one consultation to further assist you in your health and fitness goals. I'm just wondering if morning or afternoon will be easier for you to that?

If they choose morning, give them two available times. Example: I have Tuesday 9 a.m. or Thursday 10 a.m. Which is easier for you?

CLIP BOARD SHEET

Below you will find the sheet to print and place on a clipboard with a pen to keep nice and tidy. Remember to type the prospect on Friday into your prospect spreadsheet.

	Win 1 Month Free Personal Training				
	Name	Phone	Date	Booked	Comments
1					
2					
3					
4					
5					
6					
7					
8					
9					
10					
11					
12					
13					
14					
15					
16					
17					
18					
19					
20					
21					
22					
23					
24					
25					
26					
27					
28					
29					
30					

NUMBER 1 STRATEGY AS A MOBILE OR OUTDOOR PT: LEAD BOX SYSTEM

If I could now show you a simple strategy to generate (FREE) another 20-30 leads each week, would that be something that would get you excited right now?

Imagine if you walked into a café, take-away store, supplement store, fitness clothing store, or other busy store, and asked to see the person in charge.

Then you say to them: Hi, my name is Jason. I'm a successful personal trainer here locally, and just wondering how would you feel if I was to offer all your valued customers the opportunity to WIN four weeks free PT valued at $396!

OR if I was to offer all your valued customers two free PT sessions valued at $99!

What do you think most people would say? Yes, right?

By creating twenty to thirty local business relationships, you can tap into a database of thousands for little or no cost. We do this by using either acrylic plastic lead boxes or clipboards to collect people's names, so we have the power to call them and book them for a free consult. The most important part of building a business is building your database. The bigger your database, the more clients you will have.

My Top 5 Picks of Lead Box relationships
1. Takeaway Stores
2. Cafes
3. Butchers and similar stores
4. Chemists
5. Any other store that has high traffic where people wait to be served.

Here is what you say to the manager of all the above:

LEAD BOX SYSTEM 1 (WIN 1 MONTH FREE PT):

I work with a highly successful Personal Training business here locally, and was wondering how you would feel if I was to offer all your valued customers the free opportunity to go in the draw to win six free personal training sessions valued at $300 absolutely free. Is that something you would be interested in offering all your valued customers absolutely free?

LEAD BOX SYSTEM 2 (FREE TRIPLE PACK):

I work with a highly successful Personal Training business here locally, and was wondering how you would feel if I was to offer all your valued customers that spend over $50 two free personal training sessions valued at $100 absolutely free. Is that something you would be interested in offering all your valued customers absolutely free?

Of course, at this stage he/she will say yes and this will be your response: OK, if it is OK with you, this month can we run a 'spend over $50' promotion, and then next month we can place a lead box here for the prize draw, then rotate each month (one month promo, next month lead box)? This keeps it fresh.

Then say, As a token of my appreciation for servicing the lead box. which I'll clear each week and draw every three months, I'd like to offer you a free 30 minute one-on-one session for every week it is here. (This is optional).

It is vital you use this order of offers for full effectiveness. Then you call them using the given phone script found earlier in this book.

Very simple. So here you have an easy to follow step by step process to build up to five to ten businesses with alternating lead boxes and 'spend over $50' promotions. Imagine the influx of leads once you have five to ten businesses working like this.

DRAWING WINNERS

Along your Personal Training journey, you will be required to give away one month and six PT packs free, which means you will always have one free client. This will give the opportunity to someone that may not have otherwise been able to afford PT, and allows you to generate more leads. The first Monday of each month while you are having prize draws, you will draw a winner and announce them.

Here is the phone script for calling everyone who did not win:

Hi <NAME>. this is Jason, your Personal Trainer from Southlake Leisure Centre. The reason I am calling is because recently you entered the prize draw to win six free PT sessions valued at $300 at Subway. The reason I am calling is to let you know...pause... unfortunately you didn't win that prize. However, I would like to offer you a free one-hour one-on-one consultation to further assist you in your health and fitness goals. I'm just wondering if morning or afternoon will be easier for you to do that?

If they chose morning, give them two available times. Example: I have Tuesday 9 a.m. or Thursday 10 a. m. Which is easier for you?

If not interested say, We also do group training with boxing, kick pads, medicine balls, core, stretching and more on Tuesday or Thursday night. Would you prefer to come along to one of those free?

CLIP BOARD SHEET

I understand that in the beginning, buying acrylic lead boxes can be heavy on the budget. If you are on a tight budget, in the meantime you can buy clipboards for the same strategy. Create a clip board sheet to be printed and placed in the clip board, with a pen tied to a piece of string one end and the other end tied to the clip board securely.

Set twenty to thirty of these up in businesses, offering two free PT sessions OR the chance to WIN four to eight weeks free personal training. Imagine how many leads you could get!

LEAD BOX & BACKING

Here is an example of the lead box backing. You can use lead boxes for PT, bootcamp, or gym membership.

The size lead box you want is A6 Plastic acrylic with key lock.

To have them designed, I recommend www.fiverr.com

To have them printed, I recommend www.vistaprint.com

NUMBER 1 STRATEGY AS A STUDIO OR GYM OWNER:

7-Day Guest Pass System

If you own a studio or health club with memberships or even run bootcamps, then memberships are your number one focal point in your sales funnel – NOT PT. (If you don't know what a sales funnel is or don't have one yet, it will be explained later in this book). By funneling all your prospects in as members first, you will sign up more people, because it is a more affordable option. THEN you can upsell PT or other products and services. Internet marketers do this extremely well.

It's that simple—if you are not doing this yet, you are missing out on a ton of new clients.

To see an in-depth process of how this strategy works, simply visit the bonus bootcamp chapter at the end of this book.

BONUS MARKETING STRATEGIES
ULTIMATE DATABASE STRATEGY

This strategy is literally the best strategy I can think of for a brand new personal trainer. The fact is, as you read this right now, you already have 200-5000 people in your network. To reach 6 figures, you only need around 20 clients.

If you were to add all your email addresses in your contacts, phone numbers, and social media friends, how many people would be on that list? Well, this strategy is built on exposing yourself to your network fast to pick up 5-10 clients in a week or two.

Here is how this strategy works:

1) Update your ultimate database—create a spreadsheet, at the top have name, number, email and comments. In that sheet, enter every phone number from your phone, email address in your contacts, and any pre-ex forms, enquiries or clients/ex-clients. This is the beginning of your database.

2) Then we are going to use the 'first 5 strategy' and send a text message: saying 'thank you so much for your support with our personal training business (or to celebrate the launch of). As a token of our appreciation, we would like to offer the first 5 people ONLY to reply this text with your name, 2 Free PT sessions valued at $99!' Then ring all for consult pick up as clients.

There are many bulk text apps you can use. As I write this we use Group SA or ExcelSMS, which allow you to send bulk text messages.

3) Then we are going to use the first 5 strategy, and send an email. saying 'thank you so much for your support with our personal training business. As a token of our appreciation we would like to

offer the first 5 people ONLY to reply this email with your name and number, 2 Free PT sessions Valued at $99!

If you don't have email software yet I suggest using www.mailchimp. com it's great, to get started. Then as your list gets bigger, SendGrid is amazing.

4) THEN we are going to use the first 5 strategy on Facebook (personal profile and each page you have). 'Thank you so much for your support with our personal training business. As a token of our appreciation, we would like to offer: the first 5 people ONLY to Private Message this page with your name and number will receive 2 Free PT sessions valued at $99!

Very important!! WE MUST RING EVERYONE. Add them to the prospect spreadsheet found in your success blueprint, and then ring them! (Read the 7-step booking system). THIS IS WHERE WE BOOK the number of consults needed that we wrote down for our minimum target. DO NOT go home on Friday UNTIL that number is booked!

NEXT STEP TO GET 10 CLIENTS IN NEXT 2 WEEKS:

RING EVERYONE ELSE on your ultimate database and offer them a consult: Hi <NAME>, this is Jason from Your PT Expert. I'm calling you because I'm just going through a list of people that are entitled to a free Complimentary Personal Training session, and you don't appear to have had one yet. I was just wondering <NAME>, have you had your complimentary session yet? Would morning or afternoon be easier for you?

REFERRAL CAMPAIGN

There are many ways to run a referral campaign. After experimenting with many different campaigns for myself and dozens of other trainers over the last ten years, I have found the following to be the most powerful and effective. I believe, as do almost 100 providers of Personal Training Courses Australia-wide, it is important to ask for referrals. So what is the most effective way?

It is simple:

In your existing database, you will have two categories of people, prospects and suspects. Prospects are leads that haven't yet experienced personal training with you, and suspects are your active clients. This campaign is focused on your suspects. (I like to have a promotion and incentive for my prospects as well as my suspects each month).

Simply inform all your active clients via one of the following— email, text and VERY IMPORTANT also in person—that you are having a special offer this month, in which your active client will go in the draw to win one month FREE PT (Valued at $198). All they have to do is write on a piece of paper (which you supply them with) their name and two names and phone numbers of their friends/ family members who they wish to enter into the draw, to also win one month free PT.

Now you may get, well I don't know anyone... Here is how you respond:

Do you work? They say yes; then, how many people do you work with? They say 20; there are 20 already. Then, do you have family? They say yes, and you get the drift... sporting teams, church, other specific activities... Everyone knows two people. Be persistent and get the names, then don't let them take it home. Even get them to pull out their phone ...

You then place that client in the draw, and at the end of the month draw the winner, make an event out of it; even perhaps put on food and drinks etcetera, and announce the winner. Remember to have your client do their freebie as well as their existing sessions; so if they do one each week they get an extra one free each week for the month. This way it doesn't impact your income. Some of you may be thinking, this is great Jason, but what do I do with the leads?

It is simple. You simply use the referral campaign phone script below to call them and schedule them for a free comp session.

Hi <NAME>, This is Jason from South Lake Leisure Centre. I'm calling because recently <referee's name> entered you into the draw to win six free PT sessions valued at $300. So I'm calling to let you know...pause... unfortunately you didn't win that prize; however, I would like to offer you a free one hour one-on-one consultation to further assist you in your health and fitness goals, and I'm just wondering if morning or afternoon will be easier for you to that?

Now this is not cold calling because you already have a commonality... who really wants to cold call anyway?

CLIP BOARD SHEET

Below you will find the sheet to print and place on a clipboard with a pen to keep nice and tidy. Remember to type the prospect on Friday into your prospect spreadsheet.

	Win 1 Month Free Personal Training				
	Name	Phone	Date	Booked	Referred by
1					
2					
3					
4					
5					
6					
7					
8					
9					
10					
11					
12					
13					
14					
15					
16					
17					
18					
19					
20					
21					
22					
23					
24					
25					
26					
27					
28					
29					
30					

50% PROMO

If I suggested a simple strategy that, if followed, would almost double your PT sessions in just weeks, would you be interested? It is so simple that when you read the following, you will be—wow, why haven't I done this yet?

I have had many Personal Trainers run the following promotion; one trainer in particular used this technique in August and went from 22 to 38 sessions in just two weeks... almost too good to be true.

Like I said, this is so simple but when followed, extremely effective.

All you do is this:

Tell your existing clients that for this month only, they can upgrade to an extra session at only half price. E.g.: a client trains with you 1 x each week and you charge $40 for 30 minutes; you then offer that client a second session for an extra $20, being $60 each week in total.

Now you may ask, but isn't this devaluing my PT? No it doesn't, and the reason is, you obviously have spare time if you want more sessions, and in total you will boost your income by 50% immediately.

The real bonus is that after a month your clients are used to doing extra sessions with you; but here is the catch... They obviously will want to keep doing the extra session because they are achieving great results, right. But now they will have to pay you full price.

This is a win/win situation. You increase your income and your sessions, plus your clients achieve more results. This is so simple it almost seems silly, but I promise if you want more money and sessions, this is the fastest way to get a boost, especially in spring.

If you are looking for what exactly to say to a client in a session, say this:

Are you enjoying your training? Yes. Do you feel like you are getting good results? Yes. (A couple of yes sets.)

Great. As a token of my appreciation for you being so consistent, I'd like to offer you a one-off opportunity to double your results by having an extra session at half price each week for the next four weeks only. Example: if they are paying $50 for one session, then they can have another for just $25 for the next four weeks only. Now they are already paying clients and value paying full price; so why wouldn't they pay half price?

If they say no for any reason, simply say, well, I would still like to reward you, so let's do a completely free session next week. (No one will say no to this). Book them in for an extra next week, then once they have had the extra, the following week at the end of the session, ask how they are feeling after doing the extra one. Then say, I'll give you one last opportunity to have an extra session each week for half price for the next four weeks only.

SECRET WEAPON

A few years ago, I had a client who was a PT and she was lumped with a hefty tax bill. She didn't have the money, so we came up with the idea of the secret weapon to make a quick $2000-$3000 cash in the next few days.

If you create a Facebook event, do a text blast and email blast following the principles in the ultimate database strategy, and using the template below, you can easily make $600-$3000 cash bonus in the next few days:

Here is the email and Facebook event template:

<u>2 Opportunities for 2 People ONLY to Lose 10 Kilos+ with ½ Price Personal Training!</u>

GREAT NEWS: a few Personal Training time slots have opened, and I am offering 2 Lucky People ONLY (the first 2 to email *ENTER YOUR EMAIL*) the opportunity to LOSE 10+ Kilos in the next 12 weeks at HALF PRICE!

If you Act NOW and are 1 of the first 2 to email me right now, here is what you will get for ½ Price:

- 1 x 30 Minute Results-Focused Personal Training Session a week for Next 12 Weeks
- Monthly Fitness Program and Nutrition Tips
- Access to our VIP Facebook Group with Fitness, Nutrition and Motivation
- Access to our Email Newsletter subscription
- The 7 Day Raw Detox to Kick Start your Metabolism
- Measurements and re-assessments every month
- Full Tracking accountability with our online App
- 2 Free PT Sessions for a Friend or Family Member
- 2 x Free 7 Day Guest Passes to our Group Training
- 100% Money Back Guarantee: IF you stick to the program 100% you will Lose 10-20kilos

TOTAL VALUE = Almost $~~1000~~

Normal Price - $600

FIRST 2 People ONLY to quickly email me now at *ENTER YOUR EMAIL* and Live within a 20-minute drive from (NAME OF YOUR LOCATION) will get All this for JUST **$300!**

BUT you must be Quick or you will MISS OUT...

Yours in Health and Fitness

(ENTER YOUR NAME)

PS. ACT Fast, as the 2 Spots will GO VERY quickly... And if you REALLY Want to Lose that 10 PLUS Kilos this might be your only opportunity at this ridiculous price...

<u>**Secret Weapon Marketing Checklist:**</u>
- Ensure Ultimate Database is updated
- Send email Blast (make sure you use ExcelSMS and it is updated)
- Send Text Blast (Make sure you use mail chimp or email software and it is updated)
- Post on Facebook Page AND Pin to the TOP!
- Create Facebook event and invite friends
- Post on Facebook wall and promote status AND TAG all your PT Clients
- Post in VIP Group AND TAG ALL MEMBERS (Pin to the Top)
- OPTIONAL – Create Facebook offer although probably not necessary

7 STEP PROSPECT BOOKING PROCESS

Picture this: you schedule fourteen prospects for the week. You get excited and look forward to training potential new clients, then no one shows up. One of the keys to being a consistently successful Personal Trainer is to build your resilience to inconsistencies like no-shows, cancellations and losing clients. The personal trainer that can do this the most effectively and focus on what they can control will be the busier and more successful PT.

To maximize show rates and ensure we minimize cancellations, it is vital that we have a thorough booking and confirmation process.

The following process is the most effective follow-up system I have ever seen to achieve an 80%+ show rate of free consults.

What you will need:
- Your diary (I suggest Google Calendar)
- Prospect Spreadsheet open on your laptop
- Appropriate script.

1. When you call leads or prospects to schedule a comp session, use the appropriate script. This will mean you are more prepared, more organized, and have a plan. You may say, but Jason, I wish to sound natural. Well, memorize it and make it casual. The more organized you are, the better you can service your client. Have your script open on your laptop until you have memorized it. The more you stick to this process, the better your results.

2. The intention of a script is to have a planned grouping of words to increase your chances of scheduling the person in for a comp session. Once you have booked the person in your diary, also write their mobile number in. Then it is vital that once they are scheduled, you build rapport by asking three questions—how is your day, etcetera... If you hang up after the script without building any rapport, the person will feel no obligation to show to the free consult, as you have not made any contributions or deposits yourself into the relationship.

3. On the initial phone call, be sure to ask for the person's email address. Note the difference: do you have an email address? As opposed to: what is your email address? Slight changes in syntax (order of words) will make a massive difference. Statistically, if you ask a question that leads to a no answer, seventy-five percent of the time that is what you will get. Once you have their email address, type it directly into your prospect spreadsheet, and let them know you will send them an email today with the confirmation details and information. In our last fitness business, we even added a Google map of the venue in the email.

4. Now that you have the person's email address, you can invite them to become friends on Facebook. Do this the same day so they have phone contact, email contact and Facebook contact all in one day— what service. Be sure to get involved in a few of their conversations.

5. Once you are friends with them on Facebook, invite them to your Facebook VIP Group (covered in the online PT section) and post a status to welcome them.

6. Several days before, post a status on their Facebook wall saying you are looking forward to meeting them; this gets them excited and keeps you fresh in their mind.

7. The day before their meeting, RING them (not text) in the morning to confirm. If they don't answer, don't leave a message. Then ring them at lunchtime. If they don't answer this time, leave a message. If you still haven't spoken to them, ring them in the evening, or text— just confirming you received my message earlier. It is easy to assume, but perhaps they worked nine to five and had a busy day.

You may or may not be thinking, this is a bit much. But how far are you willing to go to grow your client base and offer amazing customer service, PLUS increase your show rate?

BUSINESS TRACKING

CLIENT DATABASES

The client database is a snapshot of where you are right now with your clients, and allows you to monitor how many clients you have, how much you're earning, how many sessions you have, and more. By seeing all this information on one page, it will give you more clarity and control, giving you more power over your own success. It is simple to use and is to be updated daily once you have submitted paperwork for a new client, and emailed to your team leader every Monday morning by 9 a.m. Simply add the name of the client, how many sessions they are doing each week (SPW), their contact details, which package they have purchased, the start date, if it has an end date, the amount you earn each week from them, and how often the payments are made (weekly or fortnightly)?

What constitutes an active client is someone who has completed and signed paperwork. If a direct debit client, once you have bank details and signature; if a Kick Start Pack, once money has been transferred into the company account. Once a client ceases training with you, they become an ex-client, and are moved down to the bottom of the spreadsheet and contacted regularly.

INDIVIDUAL CLIENT DATABASE

Your Individual Client Database will allow you to monitor and track how many sessions are completed and the progress of each client individually. It is important when a client asks how many sessions they have completed that we can answer that question without rummaging through our diary. Once each day, it is important to fill out new ones for these or new clients, and transfer old clients, as you will have a file for active clients and a file for existing clients. Once each day you will also update your session for the day on the individual spreadsheets.

NOTE: Remember to keep the clients in alphabetical order.

	#	Name	SPW	Email	Phone	Package	Start	End	$$ Wk	$ Frequency	Comments
Active Clients											
PT	1										
	2										
	3										
	4										
	5										
	6										
	7										
Ex Clients											
	1										
	2										
	3										
	4										

Client Database 2018

Individual Client Database						
Date:				DOB:		
Name:				Age:		
Address:						
Phone:			Email:			
Goals:						
Comments:						
Training Record						
Session #	Date	Time	Type	Comments		Action

TRACKING YOUR PERFORMANCE WITH A SUCCESS BLUEPRINT

The other day I was speaking to a young Personal Trainer, and we stumbled across the subject of what attributes make a successful PT. Many topics surfaced; marketing, sales, finances, recruitment, customer care, POD, leadership… but the hot topic seemed to be the much talked about importance of systems—an area it seems many PTs can improve on and learn more about.

After many articles, I really wanted to discuss something different in this piece, that would really strike a chord with PT business owners, and nine times out of ten, when I ask a PT, how you are tracking your results? The answer is umm… well I'm not. I find it fascinating that as PTs, we fully understand the power of tracking for our clients, yet many of us don't use it for our business.

We understand that one of the keys to success in a client that has 30, 50 or even 100kg to lose is to monitor their behaviour by tracking their food intake, exercise, and other variables. So why don't many PTs use this basic yet powerful strategy to empower their business and fast track their results?

Today a Personal Trainer asked me, what was the key to my success in having personally helped literally thousands of PTs across the globe earn a 6-figure income. After pondering for just a moment, I replied, 'The one thing each one of them had in common is they used an effective business tracking system on a weekly, monthly and yearly basis.'

Why is this such a powerful tool?

Have you ever bought a shirt or a top and then seen it everywhere you go? Or perhaps it was a car? In psychology, this is known as schema. Do you think the other shirts and cars were there previously? Of course they were; it's just they weren't in your conscious awareness yet, because it wasn't an attractor.

The first main reason tracking is so powerful is it directs your mind to focus on the right direction of your business; secondly, it increases awareness. You begin to understand exactly what is happening in your business, which in turn gives you more power and control. Thirdly, it tells you a story, a story of whether your business is on track for achieving your business objectives.

Just as if you don't know where you are going, how can you get there, if you are unaware of what is happening in your business, how can you be sure you are on track?

We have established the importance of a business tracking system; so what is the most efficient technique for proficiently monitoring our business, and how do we do it? Well the answer it is simple—through statistical analysis or stats.

Stats can be kept in the form of an Excel spreadsheet, and should include the following:
- Leads generated and retention rates
- Conversion of leads into comp sessions %
- Conversion of comp sessions into clients %
- Paid Clients Booked
- Paid clients cancelled
- Paid clients showed
- Comp sessions booked
- Comp sessions cancelled
- Comp sessions showed
- Free sessions booked (follow ups and other freebies)
- Total new clients
- Total new sessions
- Total lost clients
- Total lost sessions
- Total existing clients
- Total sessions if everyone booked in
- Income actual/received

These are just the basics, and you can utilize this in conjunction with your KPIs (Key Performance Indicators) to monitor whether your business objectives are being achieved. As you look at the above information, I'm sure you can easily begin to understand the importance of tracking your progress, and feel motivated to start monitoring your business more closely.

INDIVIDUAL STATS

Below you will find one of your most important tools for tracking your progress—your personal stats. This stat spreadsheet is one of several in a file that will be completed and updated by 9 a.m. every Monday. I call it the Success Blueprint. It is vital to your success, because it will give you the awareness you need to determine if you are on track for your goals; it acts like a video of your progress, a succession of snapshots on a weekly basis. Your team leader will help you personally with the conversions and retention; however, you will need to enter in how many leads in total you generated for the previous week, including referrals, business, new members, Facebook, and email.

Then enter how many paid PT sessions you had booked, how many cancelled, and how many showed. Your paid PT sessions are all green sessions you invoice for. Example: if you book 20 paid sessions and 5 cancel, you do 15 showed. Then do the same with your comp sessions. Free workouts are anything you are not paid for that is not a comp session, all follow ups, free prize draws, and other free sessions. Total sessions are the collection of all three categories showed tally.

New PT clients are how many new clients you gained for the week, and how many sessions are the total increase in sessions if everyone is booked. Example: if you pick up 2 clients, 1 person does 1 session and one does 2, then it would be 3 new sessions, and the same for lost clients.

Total PT clients are how many active clients you have on your database, and total sessions is how many sessions you would have booked if all clients booked in. Example: if you have 20 clients and they each do 2 sessions a week you would have 40 sessions. Income is how much money you received for the week.

On the next page you can find an example of the success blueprint spreadsheet we use with business coaching clients.

name:	Success Blueprint						
	Target	Date	Reward	Week 1	Week 2	Week 3	Week 4
Date:							
1 on 1 Clients Total	20						
PT showed sessions	40						
Total Showed PT							
GT Attendance week							
GT Sessions each week							
GT Members							
Total Income	$2000wk						
PT							
Leads generated	30						
Consults booked	14						
Consults showed	8						
New PT Clients	2						
GT							
Leads generated							
Consults booked							
Consults showed							
New GT clients							
Next Badge/Rank							
Personal goal 1							
Business goal 1							
Business goal 2							
Business goal 3							
Place of work:							

RETENTION
CONSTANTLY IMPROVE YOUR SERVICE AND ADD VALUE

I wish to challenge you. The challenge is this: What five things are you not doing in your business right now that, if you were to incorporate them, would add more value, add more revenue, and increase retention. Write them down now, then add them to your action plan. See below for more info.

50 TIPS TO IMPROVE YOUR CLIENT RETENTION USING WOW FACTORS

After including plenty of content about lead generation, marketing and growing your PT business, I thought it would make a nice change to focus on customer satisfaction and looking after your existing clients. So, you have implemented fantastic lead generation strategies and your sales are great, but for some reason, the average client only stays with you a few months. Imagine how easy it would be to grow your business if every client stayed with you for twelve months. What about three years? Some of you awesome PTs may be thinking, well my retention is already great...

Even if this is the case, there is always room for growth, and you may find some great ideas below in a collection of fifty great and simple tips to help improve your client retention. Some of these ideas you may already know, but do you do them?

There is a difference between knowing and doing, and I am also guilty of forgetting sometimes when we are so busy; it's easy to slack off a little and not go the extra mile by giving our clients 100 percent.

I hope you find some of the basics, classics and newbies below interesting enough to become even more motivated to raise the standards of PT, creating a new league of quality elite personal trainers.

After 10 years of Personal Training and 25,000 PT sessions here are the top 50 tips I have personally found work:

1) Put your existing clients before prospects.

2) Have a monthly newsletter with recognition, events, birthdays, promotions, articles and more.

3) Monitor your clients eating and training, using a diary to increase their results and give you a reference to their last session.

4) Use supplements to fast track results.

5) Celebrate birthdays with a card, text, call, email and a gift.

6) Use before and after shots to create an album to use as social proof.

7) Have a client of the month and pin them on an announcement board, give them a gift.

8) Have a client appreciation day, where you have a special day for all your clients.

9) Hold regular social events. This is great to gain referrals as well, and get their partners, friends, and families involved. Restaurants, rock climbing, bowling, Christmas parties, are just a few ideas.

10) Sell Personal Training in package form so they pay ongoing rather than having to upsell PT to renew every package.

11) Set rewards for achievements. For example, you might take them out for dinner, movies or it may be a dare, like you wear a dress next time you train them—ha!

12) Follow up on your clients occasionally to see how they felt after their session

13) Train people 1-2 x a week; that way it isn't as expensive, and when you lose clients you don't lose as many sessions.

14) Keep a ratio of 150%, for example 40 clients = 60 sessions

15) Have monthly promotions and offers for discounted PT, referral campaigns etc.

16) Hold Info evenings to educate your clients on nutrition and other health and fitness topics.

17) Focus on results. It is important to give a client what they want; if they want to lose 30 kgs, then bicep curls aren't exactly going to help.

18) Have variety in your training, keep it fresh and mix it up (stay updated on exercises and the industry).

19) Reassurance and encouragement through feedback. Let your client know they are doing great if they are, and not if not, be honest and direct.

20) Set goals and plan. Have regular goal setting sessions and ensure they reach targets.

21) Have regular reassessments of some description to show the client they are progressing.

22) Confirm all sessions. EVERY TIME!!!

23) Have prize draws.

24) Offer information relevant to their point of interest and results, including articles, books, websites and other resources.

25) Communicate your training strategy effectively, and why you have chosen that strategy.

26) Use hands on spotting, even if it is light, or body weight to maintain your kinesthetic connection.

27) Take your client out for a fresh juice or light meal after a session.

28) Give your client a personable stretch and a massage at the end of a session.

29) Have a rewards ceremony night with certificates, medallions and trophies.

30) Have group training sessions at the beach with a healthy lunch afterwards.

31) Text your clients a motivational quote of the week.

32) Encourage your client to enter a sporting event, then go watch them; example: a mini-triathlon.

33) Go shopping with your client(s).

34) Get written and video testimonials from your clients for your website.

35) Have a Facebook page or group you use to communicate with your clients regularly.
36) Hold a charity event involving your clients.
37) Make a CD of your client's favourite music and play it in their work out.
38) Organize partnership with other businesses in your area promoting a healthy lifestyle and offering discounts.
39) Train the trainer. One lucky client can win the opportunity to train you; invite all your clients to watch—they will love it.
40) If possible, sing happy birthday over the PA or to your client in front of everyone.
41) Promote charity days like red nose day, and get your clients involved.
42) Work with your clients to come up with ideas and projects to make a difference in the community.
43) Have a joke of the day/week.
44) Hold your client's towel and water bottle whilst training. I even make a joke of wiping their brow for them.
45) Buy your client a funny gift/gimmick.
46) Attend your client's special occasions like birthdays.
47) Regularly update their program with variety.
48) Ask your clients about their partner and get them involved. Offer them a free session.
49) Have your clients on direct debit so they don't link giving money and pain to you.
50) Be on time and have effective time management.

SOCIAL EVENTS

Perhaps the most powerful marketing strategy of all is social events. Not only because people don't feel like they are being marketed to, but because it creates and builds a community. Nothing increases retention like community and events.

The four main factors that influence retention are:

1. Sense of community/belonging
2. Rapport with your client
3. Results they achieve
4. Expectations met.

I truly believe you want to have two social events a month, one every two weeks.

Once a month you have a social event where you go bowling, to the pub, rock climbing, paint balling, charity event, and do something together not related to fitness. You socialize and build friendships. This also allows your clients to bond with each other. That's what a community is, when your staff and clients interact without you there. The better you achieve this, the better your sense of community and the greater your retention.

Once a month (the opposite fortnight/two weeks later) you want to have an info night or work shop. You can do an Info night on nutrition with slides, taste testing, and special guest speaker who is a nutritionist. You can also do a workshop like cross fit, boxing, TRX or other. Perhaps even a kettle bell.

If you implement this one habit into your business, you will have all your clients connect with each other, stay longer and bring a ton of referrals into your business.

Love your clients, serve them and create a fun community!

To access the Live Video of HOW to Build a 6-Figure PT Business in JUST 90 Days simply visit here → https://youtu.be/s4_8EaJAW0c

5

HOW TO BUILD A $250,000 A YEAR PERSONAL TRAINING BUSINESS IN JUST 6 MONTHS

Once you hit 6 figures in just 90 days—well, let's stop for a second. Let's say that it takes you 4, 5 or even 6 months to hit 6 figures from scratch? Will you really be disappointed? Probably not. For those that are already on 6 figures before reading this book, I still highly recommend going back and reading the last chapter, as it covers marketing, sales and other systems that will build you a strong foundation.

So, once you are on 6 figures and you have applied all the strategies in the previous chapter, we can now begin the journey to $250,000 a year ($5000 a week) within 6 months. There are several ways to do this. However, let us look at this logistically.

Step 1 is to book yourself solid. This is the number one level of business. You are self-employed and essentially own a job, because if you don't work you don't get paid. So, the first level of business is being self-employed, and what we call the security level. Now you have that security level, we want to move to the second level of business, known as the leverage level. This is where you begin to expand your business with passive income that you can forecast and predict.

Once you are booked solid and at six figures, you now have four main options:

1. Expand with semi-private personal training to consolidate and earn more per hour
2. Launch larger groups of bootcamp or group training
3. Start an online coaching or PT service of some kind
4. Hire a trainer to double your business

There really are no rules at this point, as a true fitness entrepreneur will probably desire most if not all of these services in his or her business. However, I'm personally looking for the fastest way to get you to $250,000 a year in next three months.

I have recorded a video of exactly how to do this which you can find on YouTube here: https://www.youtube.com/watch?v=lAOctHFQy7A

Once you are booked solid, to make your choice of strategies, let's look at the logistics of each.

1. Semi-private personal training. To be honest, this is my favourite of the 4 to begin with, as we go from earning an average of $100 an hour to $160 for 45 minutes. It's groups of 4 people. Here is a video of how you can build a $5000 a week fitness business just with semi-private groups: https://www.youtube.com/watch?v=zIKrnzWLnu0

   My suggestion generally is build to 40 PT sessions at $50 a session for 30 minutes, and that's your $2000 a week. Then, using a 3-week marketing campaign, we launch 10 x 45 minute semi-private personal training sessions, which increases you from $2000 a week to $3600 a week within just 4 weeks.

2. Bootcamp and group training. Personally these days I'm less inclined to choose bootcamps for several reasons. A) it usually takes you away from where you spend most your time delivering PT. B) PTs are often seduced by the income earning potential of $200-$500 an hour, which sounds great, but here is the challenge. Let's say you charge $15 per person and you can have 20 people in each group. Yes that will give you $300 an hour, but in order to gain 20 members, you will need to share your service with about 40 people, and to get in front of 40 people you will need anywhere from 100-200 leads. And there's no guarantee they will do more than 1-2 sessions a week. Imagine if you collected that many leads for PT. To reach 6 figures with PT, you only need 20 clients to make 6 figures and you would get that from 100-200 leads. So with bootcamp you would make $15,000-$30,000 a year with 100-200 leads, but with PT it's $100,000—4-5 times the amount of money for the same amount of leads and marketing.

I know it's not that simple and yes, it's more per hour, but in the early stages of your business, it's time that is your leverage and that you have more of anyway. I'm certainly not saying don't do bootcamp; I'm simply sharing the logistics after nearly eighteen years of doing this. Again, I'm looking for the fastest way to get you to $250,000 year.

3. Launching online PT. In our last OPT business we had twenty-four PTs. We have made millions of dollars online in this industry, and yes, I am a huge fan. Some challenges with online PT though: it does take up to four times longer to earn the same income. Here is why. A) You need to build a database. B) You need to connect with that database and position yourself as an expert so they will heed your advice. C) You need to add value by creating content like articles, videos and e-books, and this can take time. Plus, it requires all the same forms as a face-to-face business, but online.

Again, I'm definitely not saying don't do Online PT. I believe you should, but I would wait until you are at least at the $250,000 a year mark.

4. Hiring a trainer: Once you are booked solid at six figures, I strongly recommend either launching semi-private booking for ten sessions solid then hiring a trainer, or hiring a trainer, booking them solid with PT, and then launching semi-private. Either way it's very similar.

Here is what it may look like:

Month 1-3: build to 40 PT sessions for 30 minutes at $50 a session = $100,000 a year

Month 3-4: launch 10 x semi-private sessions with groups of 4 for 45 minutes = $3600 a week

Month 4-6: hire and build a trainer to 30 PT Sessions at $50 a session = $5100 a week

It may also look like this:

Month 1-3: build to 40 PT sessions for 30 minutes at $50 a session = $100,000 a year

Month 3-5: hire and build a trainer to 30 PT Sessions at $50 a session = $3500 a week

Month 5-6: launch 10 x semi-private sessions with groups of 4 for 45 minutes = $5100 a week

So, as you can see, its completely up to you. My suggestion is, if you are in a bigger gym with more members, I would hire a PT first, and if in a smaller gym with less members, do the semi-private first; but it honestly is up to you, as both strategies will get you to $5000 a week within six months.

HIRING A PT
RECRUITMENT PROCESS

A while back I was speaking with a fellow Personal Trainer who is enrolled in the Quantum Fitness Marketing Coaching program, and she said, 'Jason I have this problem,' and I said, 'what's the matter?' Her reply was 'well I have too many leads and too many people wanting to train with me'. I said, 'Wow that must suck having that problem... having too much business...' Realizing what she was saying she giggled.

'So what is the solution', she asked? 'It is simple to recruit a Personal Trainer to take care of the overflow.' 'Oh, but how do I do that, isn't it a costly and timely process?' I said, 'no not at all, there are seven simple steps to follow to ensure we start building a successful Personal Training team, starting with just one part-time trainer (as a contractor).'

As you read this, you may already have PTs in your business, or you may be thinking about it and not sure how to go about it, or perhaps think it may not even be for you. Either way, the following information will help you in your endeavour to grow a successful PT team, or even assist you in understanding how easy it actually is to build your team, whether it be one trainer or twenty, and you don't need to spend a lot of money.

If you are a personal trainer working on your own, I would like to invite you to flirt with the idea for just a moment...

Having single-handedly built a PT team to thirteen PTs from scratch to a $500k Annual Income in just six months, I understand the vital and essential fundamentals for successfully recruiting Personal Trainers to make our life easier, as well as to discover the holy grail of business—passive income.

Too often, as Personal Trainers, in order for us to earn more, we must work more and longer hours; you may know someone like this, perhaps intimately.

But there is an easier way you don't need to be doing 60-, 80- even 100-hour weeks. I have helped dozens of personal trainers recruit 1-20 Personal Trainers for the business with ease. You too can do so by following the simple guide below.

Step 1: Audition Process:

This part is vital for the success of your business, as it builds the foundation of your culture, driving your business towards your mission and vision. To ensure they have the right core values, ethics, belief systems, emotional intelligence, and passion, I like to use the following process.

Firstly, a phone audition to ensure they have the basic essentials like CPR, Cert 4, Insurance, registration, ABN, and any other requirements. If they have all the basic requirements we will schedule them for the first group audition.

All the potential talent that have the minimum requirements are then scheduled for a one-hour group audition to discover how they react, respond and communicate in a team environment. This part is about learning their values, emotional intelligence, and personality, to ensure they gel with you, your existing team and your business model. You might start with a few simple round robins, including about them and their background, why they became a PT, why they would be an asset to your business etcetera... Then add some challenging questions and perhaps even throw in a few team games.

I like to schedule around twelve PTs for the first group audition, and then select six from that group for a second group interview, which is about learning their technical skills. We already know they have the minimum requirements and the personality traits (in the first group audition you may use disc, Myers Briggs, VAK or other profiling to assist you); now you want to personally see their technical skills.

The way I like to do this is pair the 6 trainers up, then have them deliver a PT session for 20 minutes to their partner then swap. I also want to see how they will respond in a group situation, so I will set up 5 markers with a medicine ball each and the 6th trainer has 60 seconds to allocate an exercise for each marker, then run the circuit for 45 seconds each station without a watch. Then it will be the next trainer, but they must use different exercises and so on.

From the final 6 I will select the top 3 for a one-on-one 30-minute audition, to give them the final opportunity to convince me why they are the best person for the role.

May the best PT win. This may seem like a long and arduous process, but wouldn't you rather spend the time here rather than re-cruiting new team members every few months? Trust me, it's worth it, and they will respect you and your business even more.

Step 2: The Agreement:

It seems common practice now that the majority of PT business owners recruit ABN holders (I prefer to use the term team members or talent than contractors) rather than employees, and with good reason, as it means less paperwork and allows your team members to have a higher earning potential.

If you are choosing to have a trainer assist you in your business, and he or she is an ABN holder, it is absolutely vital you have an official agreement, even if it is fairly casual, to maintain profession-alism and to hedge your business legally.

Things to include in your agreement include: your commit-ment, their commitment, marketing, intellectual property, if/how the agreement ends, invoicing/payment process, admin and other responsibilities, branding, marketing material/equipment, and other requirements.

As I am not a qualified solicitor and it is just a template if you are ever unsure then seek out professional assistance.

Step 3: Marketing Material/Equipment:

The next step is to determine what equipment if any you will provide, and marketing materials, including business cards, flyers, welcome packs, uniform, lead boxes, signage on cars, banners, flags, and training manuals.

Depending on the invoicing/payment system, you may decide to provide all the above and pay them a smaller percentage for their work, or you may have the trainer pay for the equipment themselves. My recommendation, especially for a smaller PT business, is to provide everything yourself to ensure the quality and integrity of your business and brand; you really don't need much to start with.

Step 4: Marketing/Sales Systems:

A massive part of growing the business is your marketing and sales systems. So how do you generate your leads, and who is responsible for sales. As an example, you may choose to take responsibility for both, in which case you create and maintain all the business relationships locally, and conduct all the free consultations yourself, simply handing the new clients to your trainer.

Generally, when first starting out, it is nice to get into the habit of spending more time *on* the business and less *in* the business. That is, to take on the responsibility of generating leads yourself, then converting them, and then having your trainers take care of them while you increase your passive income.

As you grow, then perhaps give the lead generation responsibilities to the other trainer and recruit a sales manager to do all the free consultations. As your business and team grows, it is important to have minimal people selling, and your clients rotating, experiencing different trainers, so YOUR clients don't become attached to any one person, but rather to your business.

Step 5: Invoice/Payment Process:

This part is easy to overlook, but firstly, you want to determine how you will pay your trainers. As an example, I pay all my trainers for 50% of the sessions they deliver, and my head trainer an additional 10% of all profits for their sales and admin efforts.

Some people even use sliding scales or probation periods. I'm not a big fan of commissions because it chips into profit margins too much and doesn't really create the team environment I want.

Once you determine the rate, it is important to create a tracking system and invoicing system, so your trainer may invoice you weekly, in which case you cross reference all their sessions with the direct debit reports and signed sessions. Trust is not enough, especially as your business grows, as people make mistakes. Having all clients sign either the trainer's diary or cards ensures consistency and balancing of your books.

Step 6: Training/Meetings:

The audition is just the first step. From there, if a team member does something you don't like, you have no one to blame but yourself, as you put them there. It is then important to have consistent communication to ensure your team grows with your business personally as well as professionally.

I like to have a team business development meeting once a month, a team adventure once a month, like white water rafting, weekly inspiration every Monday, and a one-on-one meeting weekly. Again, this may seem like a lot of meetings but guarantees the necessary communication and growth of your team.

Step 7: Business Tracking/Admin/Reporting:

The key to progression is monitoring; just like we do with our clients, it is the same with our business. So every Monday, I have all stats, updated lead sheets, database, goals, projections, budgets and other necessary reports emailed to me by the required team member. Generally, it depends on the system you are using, and whether they are responsible for generating leads and sales.

So here you have it: seven simple steps to creating or growing your existing successful team.

I hope this gives you deeper insight into some specific strategies to help your business grow exponentially.

ADVERT EXAMPLE

Here is an example of what your advert may look like:

Head Personal Trainer - Your PT Expert

Are You a Personal Trainer Looking to Get Booked Solid, Make Good Money and Grow Within an Organization?

Your PT Expert is a rapidly growing department of Your PT Australia with Your PT Coach— Helping PTs Australia-wide to build their business, and Your PT Web—logos and websites designed specifically for PTs, and Your PT Massage launching VERY SOON!

Your PT Expert has 3 venues in Perth and is looking for a Head PT with great leadership skills.

The successful PT will conduct personal training sessions and be responsible for assisting with recruitment and business operations within the club, and secure relationships with local business, with the opportunity to move up into higher management, and eventually, as a coach, to coach PTs Australia-wide to build their business. Other opportunities include upper management and massage.

Certificate IV in Fitness is required as well as Insurance, First Aid, CPR, registration and ABN.

Values required; Loyal, honest, focused, driven, caring, team player, results-focused, ambitious, open minded, hard working, and enjoys social events and working with charities.

This is a unique position unlike any in Australia. With a very high demand, and as a member of a company that has rapid growth in several areas, you will have a great opportunity to earn top $$$, grow as a person, learn invaluable business skills, and move up the organizational structure.

Good luck :)

CEO
Jason Grossman
jason@yourptexpert.com

To see a video recording of the entire seven step process for recruiting the right trainer and team, you can watch it here on YouTube: https://youtu.be/Hi58KbU0E2E

TIME MANAGEMENT

One of the biggest challenges I see fitness business owners faced with at this stage of their business, besides the psychology necessary for transitioning from a PT to a real business owner and learning to let go, is time management. At this stage, we are so crazy busy working 60-80 hours a week, it can be challenging to be organized with our time and productive.

Below I have added two strategies that will allow you to begin to control and master your own time. If you apply them, you will squeeze more juice out of life and grow your business with more productivity.

In order to grow your business, you'll need to carve up 10–20 hours a week out of your busy schedule. Considering that you are probably working 40–60 hours, this may be difficult, but shouldn't be impossible. Once you have some time to invest in team building and marketing, you'll see your business begin to grow. Let's find out where your time is going.

1. Fill in the chart below to estimate how much time you spend per day of the typical week working in your business:

Day of the week	Hours
Monday	
Tuesday	
Wednesday	
Thursday	
Friday	
Saturday	
Sunday	
Total =	

2. Fill in the chart below with the 5-10 tasks categories you do on a weekly basis. E.g. PT, classes, travel, admin (paperwork/emails/payroll) phone calls etc...

Task	Hours
1 Sessions	20-30 hours (10 hours coaching)
2 Marketing	10-15 hours
3 Sales	14 hours (consults)
4 MLM	15-20 hours (lunch and evenings 2-3 hours/Saturday 6-8 hours)
5 Phone calls	4-5 hours – Monday and Friday
6 Finances/tracking	Monday 1 hour and Friday 1 hour
7 Date night and date/family day	Saturday night and Sunday all day
8 Training and nutrition	5-10 hours week
9 4 x rituals (includes 1 hour day PD)	See webinar on YouTube
10 Travel?	
Total =	Total Hours = 80 hours business

Rework and refigure the numbers in these tables until the total hours in both tables are approximately equal. This will give you a good picture of what tasks are consuming most of your time. Now choose the one or two task categories that can be delegated.

I will then help you to put together a detailed schedule, saving time, being able to delegate unwanted tasks, and hiring new staff.

We will also analyze each category to see where we can make positive changes.

IDEAL WEEK

Some people say the most powerful skill to master is time management. Of course we cannot manage time, but we can manage ourselves and what we do with our perceived time. To know what we want, then to have the discipline to do what is necessary to achieve those things, is one of the most important skills of all, and again as written previously in this manual, the first step is awareness.

Have you ever felt as though there is too much to complete in just one day or week? Or wished there were more hours in a day or more days in a week? Then this next process will give you the clarity and insight to choose what you want to do by making sure you are in control of your actions and time, and not the other way around. Having an Ideal week will mean you can be more productive, achieve more, have better time management, earn more money, choose to do what you want when, and give you more clarity and organization.

On the next page, you will see an example of an ideal week, and on the following page is a template for you to begin creating your ideal week. Start by determining the larger items of time; for example, how many hours of PT you wish to do, how many hours of training, your times off etcetera. Remember you are creating this based on where you want to be, not where you are now. This will give you something to focus on, driving you forward with clear vision. Specifically as a PT you will let your clients know where they can train, not the other way around which will help you consolidate your sessions more effectively.

What you may include:

PT
Your own training
Admin and phone calls
Office time
Meetings
Travel
Sport
Showers/food
Reading

In personal training, cancellations and no-shows can seem like a burden, but when you have your ideal week set up, they can be used productively. For example, as I always used to do 60-70 sessions each week, I relied on my cancellations to squeeze my own workouts in, do admin, or call prospects and clients. The more you use this strategy and make a habit of asking yourself the question, what I could be doing more productively with my time right now? the more you will benefit from this process.

To see a video recording of exactly how to use these tools, checkout our time management video on YouTube here https://youtu.be/ HzIAmNxHyIU

6

THE FIRST 7-FIGURE FITNESS BUSINESS I BUILT

I had been doing personal training for eight years at the same gym, doing 60+ sessions week in week out. No breaks and no holidays. I loved it there BUT it was time for a change. I was offered an opportunity to be a fitness director for the first ever GoodLife Health Clubs (a large chain in Australia) in Western Australia, and the potential of the role was exciting.

I said yes to the role, and as the gym was still being built, I began to do interviews for the personal training team. Our goal was to hire a team of eight PTs. We advertised on a website called Seek, which is the largest job seeking site in the country, looking for JUST 2 Personal Trainers to increase the exclusivity of the role.

We received over 100 resumés, and so I began the process. I made the mistake of doing the interviews one-on-one, and only had the opportunity to meet them once before deciding, and because the gym was not yet operational I did not get to see them perform either. I cannot remember exactly how many interviews I did, but it was a lot, and the process took several weeks.

The gym finally opened and the open day was a huge success. I had created a roster with pre-booked consults, PT and group consults to squeeze in as many people as possible and maximize our sales on the day. As we had eight trainers, we had plenty of leverage.

We then had all the trainers hit the phones and ring all the members to book them in for their free consults and upsell them PT.

As the Fitness Director, I would have a one-on-one meeting with each of the trainers weekly and a team meeting monthly. I had been the head trainer at my previous gym for a while and had some success. Within six months we smashed the records of the other thirty-three clubs in the country at the time, more than doubling the sales of the next highest club for personal training.

I was contacted by the C.O.O. at the time, who wanted clarity as to what I was doing and why our sales were so high. I explained to him we used a weekly tracking system so all trainers knew their targets of sessions, consults and their conversion rates. We then ensured all scripts and sales training sessions were very regular.

In fact, that's when I realized that here I was working my ass off for a few hundred dollars a week, making another company nearly $750,000 a year, when I could be doing that for myself. Don't get me wrong—I'm very grateful for that opportunity, and I learned so much from that company and their amazing systems. BUT after nearly a decade in someone else's gym, I was ready for something much bigger.

I had no idea what I was going to do or what I wanted to do, and I pretty much spent the next six months on a couch not doing much at all except contemplating. One day I was reading a book called the *Power of Now* by Eckart Tolle, a spiritual leader and bestselling author. I have been a huge fan of personal development for some time, reading hundreds of books, listening to thousands of audios, and honestly cannot tell you how many courses and seminars I've done, but I can tell you I've spent nearly half a million dollars on them.

It was while reading this book I had an idea. An idea to coach Personal Trainers to build a 6-figure PT business. I had been doing it for myself and other trainers for nearly a decade and I knew I was very good at it.

Literally that day, I thought of a name: Your PT Coach. I got a cheap tacky logo from a free logo design and created a Facebook group. I started adding 50-100 PTs a day as Facebook friends (back when they didn't block you LOL), and added them to our coaching group. Within just months, from the clients I had, I was making over $300,000 a year, and realized I was onto something. Side note: when I did this, I had no content, no actual program. Nothing really rock solid. I just knew, with my knowledge and skills I could help PTs.

About six months in was when I realized we needed an office space. So, I hired a personal assistant and internal designer and IT person, and we moved into this tiny office about the size of a bedroom. We started having trainers ask for logos and websites, so we launched Your PT Web, where we designed logos and websites for PTs that actually worked. Then all of a sudden we had a lot of people asking us for PT and bootcamp, as that was the bulk of my database.

Now this is the part you might find interesting; Reluctantly I decided to launch a PT Business called Your PT Expert. I didn't want to be a part of it personally, so I placed an advert on Seek for a State Personal Training Manager, and started at the top.

This time we did it the smart way. We used a four-step audition process:

Step 1): We rang everyone we received a resumé from on a Thursday and Friday and booked them in for a group audition Monday at 1 p.m. If they couldn't make this time, we would not meet with them outside of this session, as we had a funnel to ensure we found the right trainer and best candidate. I never look at resumés, as all you will find on there is what the person who wrote it wants you to know. We would book everyone in for the first group audition, as we wanted big numbers, and this makes the opportunity look more desirable to people, and they will value it more and work harder to get it.

Step 2): Monday at 1 p.m. we delivered a group audition. Side note: The reason I call it an audition rather than interview is that Interview is employee language. I'm not looking for employees, I'm looking for business minded people who want to come and learn from me for two, three or five years, then go and run their own business. I would rather they feel like business partners with me, then they will be more passionate. I don't call it a job description, I call it a talent description.

In the group audition, we did a round robin asking a series of questions to determine their beliefs and values and see how they interact socially. I believe these three things are more important than technical skill or ability, which are things you can teach.

To see exactly how we do this process you can watch our YouTube Video here: https://youtu.be/Hi58KbU0E2E

Step 3): after the first group audition I informed the group of at least eight people that we would contact them all later that day to let them know which fifty percent of them had made it through to the next round. And scheduled them in for Wednesday at 1 p.m. for the practical audition. In this audition, I had them pair up and train each other one-on-one for twenty minutes, then swap. To be honest, I looked to see how they reacted to being trained rather than actually training. To me the least important thing is a PT's technical ability, which may sound strange, but it literally takes a few minutes to correct form, while attitude, on the other hand, is a different story.

After the one-on-one, I wanted to see them perform in a group setting, so if there were six people, I set up six cones. I appointed one of the trainers to be the group trainer, and the others stood on a cone to be trained. The trainer had sixty seconds to let each person know what stations they were to do for sixty seconds. This shows how they think on their feet in a group setting. Then when it was the next trainer's turn, they had to choose different exercises. Once they had all had a go, I would be the trainer and smash them—LOL!

Step 4): At the end of the second group audition I informed them I would contact each of them later that day to let them know which two would make it through to the final round on Friday—a one-on-one with me. In this session, it was just them and me, and I took them through the PT Agreement so they understood the role 100%. Then they had one last chance to convince me why we should choose to hire them.

In my career and businesses, I have had almost 100 PTs in my employment, team or business in some way; this process is the most thorough I've ever seen for finding the right trainer, and I still use it.

Going through this process, we found a state Personal Training Manager, and he was amazing. I had written an eighty-page operations manual for him, as he was going to run the business. I would have a one-hour meeting with him on Monday and a thirty-minute meeting with him on Friday and he would do everything. I simply trained him using the manual.

That week I had him set up thirty lead boxes to win six free PT sessions valued at $300, and the following week we generated several hundred leads from them. He simply hit the phones and rang them all and booked them in for consults. We had organized an exclusive relationship with a recreation centre just near our small head office, and he could deliver it there. He had his business cards and uniform, and off he went.

He was paid a $300 a week base. He wasn't paid for delivering consults, but for every consult he sold, he received a $99 commission. This $99 was simply added as a kick-start fee to all new clients' payments, so the client covered the cost.

Within literally weeks he was doing 40 paid sessions a week. The business charged clients $50 for 30 minute sessions (but we sold them in package form), and we paid the trainer $20 + $2 GST for each session. Many trainers making the mistake of paying their trainers 50% gross income to trainers. It's important to pay 50% net, as the business incurs many more fees than the trainer.

He asked if we could hire another trainer, and since I was working literally 1.5 hours a week on the business and he completely ran Your PT Expert, I said why not. Within just months there were three trainers and the business was making over six figures net. To clarify, I was putting over $100,000 a year in my pocket for working 1.5 hours a week. This was exciting. We expanded our locations to three locations, appointed a head trainer at each location additional to the state PTM, and within less than eighteen months, we had nine trainers booked solid or near booked solid, doing over 300 sessions a week and I was still only working 1.5 hours a week.

This leg of the business was putting more than $200,000 net profit a year in my pocket after everything including tax, all for 1.5 hours a week. We had also outgrown our old office and upgraded to a much larger office with seventeen of us. We had business coaches, nutritionists, personal trainers, designers, a personal assistant, and myself. Business was booming. We were taking more than $1.2 million a year in just eighteen months from scratch, no loans, and no money down.

I then went and did something crazy... I feel in love with the girl of my dreams at the age of thirty-three. I was living in Perth, Western Australia, and she was living in Brisbane on the east coast. I decided to go all in for love and shut down the company, Your PT Australia, and let all my staff go. I broke the lease on my office, gave all my belongings to my family and charity, and moved over to Brisbane to be with her, with just a suitcase in hand.

It was a big risk, but five years on it was one of the best decisions of my life...

7

THE SECOND 7-FIGURE FITNESS BUSINESS I BUILT

I had just moved to Brisbane on the east coast of Australia. I went from an income of $25,000 a week down to $297 a week, and into $218,000 debt, to go all in for love. It was a tough time, because at the time I was also diagnosed with glandular fever and chronic fatigue. I had made a promise to my sweetheart Kailey we were going to create an amazing life, one that most people can only ever dream of. The problem was I was bedridden. So, the only thing I could think of at the time was to lie in bed with my laptop and build an online business.

Many people ask why I did not sell my previous business, and the answer was an easy one for me. We had built a database of near half a million people, and if I had sold that business, to start again would be much harder. To this day, it was an intelligent decision, as otherwise I might not be writing this book.

My debt repayments were meant to be $2000 a week, but I was only earning $297 a week, so needed to act fast. Lying in bed, I launched a ridiculously cheap online PT service and a ridiculously cheap business coaching service; instead of $99 or $69 a week it was just $29!

Because I had drastically decreased our price and profit margins, a ton of people flocked to the two services. Within four weeks I was making over $2000 again, but was still bed ridden, and the problem is, as you may be aware if you offer a cheap price, you may attract cheap clients.

Once I hit the six figures and had my debts re-covered, I put our prices back to the normal rate. Within three months I was back to earning over $300,000 a year from Online PT Clients and business coaching clients that were personal trainers. I was now booked solid and looking to expand through leverage of automatic websites and new coaches and teams. I launched a product called the 7-day raw detox, which took three months to create. It was just $49, but was a completely automated program.

When it launched, we were blown away by its success. It was selling thirty to forty a day, bringing in $1500-$2000 A DAY of passive income, and continued to do so for months. Due to the success of this program, we also launched one called the 8 Week Body Blitz. We barely sold a thousand of them at $69. This just proves we can never truly know how well something will sell.

We launched several automated programs for PTs, including a business kit, a social media program, and a 6-figure program, all completely automated, and set up affiliates for all these, and the passive income was amazing.

As great as all of the products were, they will never truly set you free, because it's impossible to forecast guaranteed income. You might sell one thing one day then 100 the next. Ever tried to live on an inconsistent income?

I believe most online trainers fail because of this delusion that you can forecast your income from selling products. One of the reasons why personal training is so successful as a business model is the direct debit system. Due to direct debit, you can forecast exactly how much you will earn each week based on your current clients, and get paid in one lump sum each week. This creates certainty and, to a point, some security.

It was at this point I truly understood that if you want to make a living 100% online, that you need forecasted income from memberships, subscriptions or coaching. Some kind of regular income.

So, this is where we began to build our coaching team. We built five business coaches to coach Personal Trainers, and didn't just focus on business, but now focused on creating a business that supported the lifestyle trainers seek.

I created an affiliate program for trainers wanting to go online, where for $99 a week we gave them everything they needed to run a successful online PT business, including websites, fan pages, manuals, marketing, systems—literally everything. And using this model, we built to twenty-four online Personal Trainers.

In addition to all that, we were aligned with a nutrition network marketing company that was also bringing in six figures, and within just nine months of moving to Brisbane (six months of that time in bed) we had created an income for the business of over one million a year and financial freedom.

We had a team of nearly seventy people in seven countries with business coaching for PTs, online PT, life coaching, and so many products and affiliates I lost count. Life was good—it was really amazing.

We then spent two and a half years straight living out of hotels, travelling to sixteen countries, ticking off over 230 bucket list items, launching a kid's charity, and writing my first book, *From the Streets to a Millionaire!*

Now, nearly six years on from leaving Perth and launching this business, we keep life very simple. We only sell products, books and services that legitimately impact people's lives in a massive way.

Our primary business is coaching; we have an amazing team of coaches growing very rapidly. In fact this month alone, we have recruited five new coaches to deal with so much work coming in. January 2018, we generated nearly 2000 leads for the month to book in for coaching.

1. Quantum Body Transformation Coaching
2. Quantum Fitness Marketing
3. Quantum Life Coaching and Wealth Coaching
4. A Travel Network Marketing Business

My purpose in life is to help one million people live the life of their dreams, so if it doesn't help people do that, we do not offer the product or service. We literally a few weeks ago hit the $2 million a year mark and forecasted to hit $5 Million a year by December, and that doesn't include our investments, book sales or network marketing business, which is also thriving.

As we teach in all our programs, we fuel our financial freedom accounts to invest in new businesses and property each year, and spend time travelling, ticking off bucket list items, and serving others. I'm publishing two more books this year, doing a lot more public speaking and charity work.

We truly have been able to create a life most people dream of, and simply want to help as many people now do the same.

It is possible for you to do what you love and have a thriving fitness business and still travel and have a work life balance. I know that as you keep reading this book and applying the principles, as you expand your belief about what is possible, you too can live the life of your dreams.

8

HOW TO BUILD A 7-FIGURE A YEAR FITNESS BUSINESS IN JUST 12 MONTHS

At this stage of your business, you have built a minimum gross income of $250,000 a year forecasted direct debit. This is where it gets truly exciting, as you move from level two of business, the manager level of leverage, to the third level of business, true business owner and financial freedom.

You have begun to tap into your four types of leverage: people, time, money and resources. To make the transition from $250,000 a year to over $1,000,000 a year, we really need to ramp up the number of people in your business, automated systems, and also your marketing and advertising budget.

WHAT NEXT?

You currently have one trainer and yourself, delivering around eighty PT sessions and ten to fifteen semi-privates.

HERE IS YOUR NEXT STEP:

The fastest way to get you to seven figures in the next six months is to advertise again, but this time for two personal trainers; here is why.

When you hire your first trainer, they are hungry and excited because they are your first, they feel special. When you hire your next trainer, for obvious reasons, they won't get that same attention or feeling. They just won't, no matter how much we look after them, because they know they are not the only trainer. By hiring two trainers this time, they will become running bodies and form a special bond (if you pick two that will work together well). Also, at this stage you are getting busier, so when you train them you can send them off to train each other and do role play together, saving you more time. Thirdly, they will create friendly competition to see who can get more clients faster and catch up to your first trainer. It's all psychology. Lastly, let's say you hire one trainer and one quits, you are stuck where you cannot grow. If you hire two, you will have more momentum in your business. Now you can gain more clients faster than when it was just you, because now there are four people selling in your business.

Once you have grown all three of those trainers to at least twenty to thirty sessions, giving you 100 sessions, it's time to take the next step and automate your business.

IMPORTANT: I see many business owners, at this stage of their business, stop doing consults and selling PT. But let me ask you this. Who will market and sell your business best? You will, right? So, until your business is automated, it is your responsibility to hit your sales targets, since you can control that. Then anything our trainers gain is a bonus. Make sense?

For example, as I write this, we have eight coaches. Due to consolidation and relaunching our company, I do not currently have a 2IC, so I run the business. Our growth target at this stage is six new coaching clients a week. Therefor it's my number one job to gain six new clients myself.

SIDE NOTE: The above sentence was written just a few months ago, and we now have eight coaches selling, doing 100 consults a week and averaging fifteen new clients a week. That's an increase of six figures a week and increasing fast!

Even though there are nine of us in the business selling, the responsibility is mine, as this will guarantee I hit my targets. This is HUGE, and I hope you get this.

If all I do is get six new clients a week personally, in twelve months from now, we would have increased our direct debit income by $1.5 million dollars a year.

Now here is the exciting part: we book ten consults a week with those eight coaches; that means they are booking eighty consults a week, so we both know we will gain many more clients than six. This is a clever hedging strategy to avoid the frustration of relying on others to build your business for you too early, and it guarantees you hit your targets.

If you and your three PTs book ten consults a week each, that's forty prospects, and all you need is to gain four new clients a week to hit $1 million a year. Good odds, right?

So, gaining four new clients a week is your personal goal; everything else is a bonus.

THE TWO THINGS YOU WILL NOW NEED TO BUILD TO 7 FIGURES

In this transition period you will also recruit a 2IC, a manager, or someone to run the business for you. They will take care of day-to-day operations, be in charge of sales and marketing, and also of training and recruitment.

In fact, there are only really two things you need, when done right, to make this big transition:

1. A complete operations manual of everything and anything in your business. Sales systems, scripts, marketing strategies, tracking, training and recruitment, financial systems, and more.

2. A person you can teach this manual to who will follow the system 100% and ensure everyone else in the business does also.

You may remember how I launched my PT Business (Your PT Expert) when I shared my story earlier. I simply hired a State PTM and gave them a manual, and had a one-hour meeting with them on a Monday and a thirty-minute meeting with them on a Friday.

At this stage of your business, there should already be systems in place to ensure fifty to one hundred leads every week, and a recruitment strategy to continue the growth of your team, and finally a plan for expansion of venues to allow for the growth.

If this is the case, then now is the time we advertise on Seek and hire a manager. I don't personally like the term manager anymore, as people don't want to be managed, they want to be led, and they desire opportunities to lead.

Regardless of the title you give this person who will run the business, here are some insights to consider for their role:

MAIN ROLE AND RESPONSIBILITIES

- Ensure all systems and procedures in all PT manuals, including state PTM, Head and Master PT manuals, are followed in their entirety
- The launching of and distribution of responsibilities for all marketing plans, sales funnels, website and Facebook plans
- State tracking spreadsheets including database and stats
- Email database and monthly newsletter
- Recruitment
- PT meetings and training
- Achieving sales targets
- Filing and registrations
- Creating relationships with and setting up new venues for Personal Trainers

- Ensuring targets and KPIs for Your PT Expert are met.

When recruiting for this person, there is a great chance you will hire internally. Meaning you will choose someone who has proven themselves already in your business. However, I make everyone work for it, so I always stick to the process. I advertise on Seek (if in Australia), use the four-step audition process, and invite all my current team into the interviews/auditions.

There is a good chance I will hire internally (not always) but I still want them to appreciate and value the role by going through the entire experiences. It also teaches them the importance of them sticking to the systems.

Once you have a Manager/Head PT/State PTM/ Team Leader /C.O.O. or whatever label you choose, take them through a four-week training development program, which is also likened to a probation period.

Here is an example of a training program we used to use:

| | | | Completed Signed | |
		Page#	Team Leader	PTM
Week 1	Sign 2 agreements			
	Hand them certificate - laminated			
	Distribute State PTM handbook			
	Order 500 business cards; transfer all files onto PT's laptop			
	Add State PTM to work on Facebook profile			
	Record voice mail			
	Create Expert email address and web profile			
	Filing and in tray systems			

	Shadow team leader for 1-on-1 PT meetings			
	Texting each day, organizing Hour of Powers and emailing team leader each Monday			
Week 2	Invoicing process			
	Master stats, prospects and client database			
	Explain meeting procedures and agendas			
	PT awards system			
Week 3	Qualifications and insurance tracking			
	1/31 tracking			
	Complete monthly goal spreadsheet			
	12 week marketing plan			
	Growth budgets and KPIs			
Week 4	Discuss monthly goal spreadsheet and complete			
	New ideal week			
	Facebook plan			
	Recruitment process			

OPERATIONS MANUAL

By the time you have your manager ready to run the business, it is important to have not only their role description ready, but also an operations manual for all PTs. In our coaching program, we actually offer you an eighty-two-page template, which literally took me nearly 100 hours to write. This could save you a lot of time.

In the meantime, here is the ten-week training development program your new manager will take all new PTs through, which forms the base of the manual:

				Completed Signed	
			Page#	Team Leader	PTM
Week 1	Collect copies of CPR, insurance, Cert 4, Registration, ABN and bank details then file				
No PT	Sign 2 agreements				
	Hand them certificate - laminated				
	Distribute PT handbook				
	Order 2 shirts and 500 business cards; transfer all files onto PTs' laptops				
	Add Expert to work on Facebook profile				
	Add as an admin to Facebook groups				
	Record VMB	4			
	Invite all friends to Expert group				
	Create Expert email address	4			
	Shadow at least 10 hours with another PT comps/PT				
	Taken through a workout by team leader				
	Office and gym housekeeping/ professionalism	4			

	Diary colour coding and process – mark times	5		
	Phone call training booking process and scripts	6		
	Book min. 14 prospects for next week (give leads spreadsheet). Have 10 booked by Friday			
	Comp session process and training	9		
Week 2	Prospect spreadsheet and 4-week cycle	24		
Start Comps	Business relations training - systems and spreadsheet	28		
	Explain meeting procedures and timetable	35		
	Add to superstars board and explain	37		
	Texting each day and Hour of Power	37		
	Invoice process for start-up	38		
	Comp process revision – talk team leader through process			
Week 3	Client databases and stats	40		
Start PT	Paysmart system	46		
	Complete monthly goal spreadsheet	46		
	Launch floor walking competition – 20 names	48		
	Write personal profile	50		
	Comp process training and revision (Memorized)			
	Personal mission	51		
	Tracking for clients	52		

Week 4	Discuss monthly goal spread-sheet and complete			
	Record video profile; take photo in uniform and upload to website with written profile in team section	50		
	1/31 System	53		
	Order profile board for club	53		
	Bank account and tax training			
	Take team leader through a workout			
	Ordering system	55		
Week 5	Supplement training and set up account	56		
	Facebook lan – explain and start using	58		
	Discuss monthly goal spread-sheet and set timeframe with dates for goal sessions and conversions			
Week 6	Finalize monthly goal spreadsheet			
	Discuss Ideal week process and complete	59		
	Start using Facebook plan effectively with accountability			
	Referral campaign training and launch	64		
	Wow factors and retention	65		
Week 7	Discuss tracking of monthly goal spreadsheet			
	Life wheel: explain and complete	67		
	Discuss completed Ideal week			
	Comp process training and revision			

Week 8	Explain vision board	69			
	Track Ideal week				
	Take team leader through a workout				
	50% off promo training and launch	69			
Week 9	Budgeting process and spreadsheet	71			
	Organize bookkeeper and accountant				
	Comp process revision and overcoming objections				
	Discuss completed vision board				
Week 10	Projections spreadsheet and have ready for week 11	73			
	P & L spreadsheet and have ready for week 11				

This also serves as a checklist to ensure effective communication and training of all new teams.

YOUR TARGETS

So, you have built to $250,000 a year. You have three PTs, have created an operations manual and hired a manager. What's next?

Your primary focus is training that manager to be the best they can be; his number one role is sales and marketing manager. So ensuring he or she hits the marketing and sales targets is most important. In the first few months, you may have to get your hands dirty, but once they are trained properly, it will literally only take you a few hours a week, and you can have the freedom to do what you want when you want. Spend more time training yourself, choose how much PT you wish to do by choice, maybe travel, write that book you have always wanted, do that charity fund raiser, or spend more time with family.

YOUR TARGETS FOR REACHING 7 FIGURES WITHIN NEXT 6 MONTHS

At the $250,000 mark, you will basically have yourself and another PT doing 70-80 sessions a week, and 10 semi-privates.

Now we hire 2 more personal trainers and repeat the process.

Each trainer has: 40 PT + 5 x SP (semi-private) sessions = Just over $2500 a week gross from each trainer.

If you do 20 PT sessions a week ($1000 a week) and 5 SP sessions ($800 week) and combine the income, this will give you around $8000-$9000 gross a week.

Month 6-7 is where we hire two new trainers.

Month 7-9 is where we book them solid, increasing by 60 PT sessions (30 clients) in 8 weeks.

Month 8-9 is where we hire a manager and we have around $8000-$9000 income.

Month 9-10 is where we hire 2 more trainers and book them solid, adding $4000.

Month 11-12 is where we hire 2 more trainers for total of 8, each bringing in around $2,500 a week each, by delivering 40 x PT sessions and 5 x SP sessions.

8 PTs delivering 30-40 sessions = 250-300 PT sessions/$12,50–$15,000 a week.

6 PTs delivering 5 SP sessions = 30 SP sessions/$4500.

Let's be honest for a moment. Are these big numbers? Yes! Is it likely it will go to plan exactly following these numbers? Probably, not. BUT what it does do is give you a map to follow, with targets to aim for.

This is just an example of a way to get to seven figures. In my personal opinion it's the fastest. Does this mean you have to follow this plan exactly? Of course not, but if you want speed, this is the fastest way we have found.

EXCITING NEWS: The above only includes PT & SP (semi-private), and truthfully, an ambitious entrepreneur like yourself wanting a 7-figure business won't just have two income streams; you will also probably implement some or all of the following along this journey:

1. Online PT, packages, products and services
2. Bootcamp and larger groups including classes
3. Workshops and challenges
4. Supplements, merchandise, clothing and equipment
5. Network marketing products.

So, let's break these down:

ONLINE PT

You may be wondering, where does Online PT and income come in and when? Here is my suggestion, after making millions of dollars online. Wait until you have a 2IC. Once you have someone in charge, you can focus on building your online business, service, or empire. We can definitely assist you with this if you like. The reason is, it does take up a fair amount of time in the beginning, and there are no guarantees for success.

BOOTCAMP

As I mentioned earlier, I'm not a huge fan of bootcamp when wanting to build fast and aggressive, which is what this book and plan is about. It takes time. Even if we do it fast, you are looking at a minimum of six months before you make six figures. So if you do wish to implement bootcamp, my suggestion is, do it at the $250,000 mark.

WORKS SHOPS & TRANSFORMATION CHALLENGES

These are a great way to generate leads and build business. Typically, most trainers seem to use them for add value and making a quick buck, which is fine, but again, we want to stay focused on our rapid plan towards seven figures in twelve months. My personal suggestion here again is, wait until you have a 2IC.

SUPPLEMENTS & MERCHANDISE

I have seen some PT businesses looking really amazing on the surface, with t-shirts, shakers, towels, etcetera, but there is not a lot of money in them, and they can be a distraction unless you have a big business. Again, I'm not saying don't do these, for as an entrepreneur you will probably have all of these things in your business. My suggestion would be, wait until you are seven figures or at least have a 2IC. Until then, if you wish to promote supplements, I would simply find a partner to save you the time. We want to send most of your time building to the seven figures fast!

NETWORK MARKETING

I understand many people have a bad taste about network marketing This book is not a network marketing book. Although I am a massive fan of network marketing. Because, let's be honest, you won't have your current fitness business forever, so what's your retirement plan? (By retirement I mean post-fitness days).

I usually get my guys to align with a network marketing company once they are on six figures, because you will be talking to people anyway, so it doesn't have to take much time, and you can speed up your residual income faster by getting paid for those conversations you will have anyway.

SALES FUNNEL TARGETS

As you read the targets, you may think and feel there is something missing. You have the 'what' to do, but what about the 'how'?

If the what is the above targets and KPIs, the how is the strategies we will use to get there.

The first part of this is the weekly targets required for each stage.

If stage 1 is 6 figures in 90 days, these would be our targets:

Generate 30 leads

Book 14 consults

Deliver 8 showed consults

Gain 2 new clients.

It's important to note that gaining two clients is an increase of two clients for the week, so if you lose a client one week, that week you will require three new clients to hit your target.

The above numbers will give you 24 clients from scratch in 90 days, and 40 sessions. $50 x 40 = $2000 a week/$100,000 a year. Six figures!

Stage 2 is $250,000 a year within the next 90 days (6 months from day 1). For this, your sales funnel targets would be as following:

Generate 30 leads

Book 14 consults

Deliver 8 showed consults

Gain 2 new clients

These targets are the same as stage 1, as we are simply doubling our PT; then we will launch our semi-private service, using a three-week marketing campaign and launch week. At the end of that four weeks, you will have at least close to ten SP sessions booked solid, based on the marketing plan, so it won't change the above sales funnel targets.

Stage 3 is moving from $250,000–$1,000,000 in the next six months. This seems like a massive jump, but only in the mind. Because here you have more money to leverage, more time to leverage, and more people selling in your business, so you will begin to experience compounding and exponential growth.

At stage 3, your sales funnel targets are as follows

3a) You hire your third and fourth trainer. At this stage, you will now have four people selling in your business. And you want everyone booking at least ten consults each, so here are your numbers.

Generate 100 leads
Book 40 consults
Deliver 24 consults
Gain 4 new clients a week.

These numbers may seem a little obscure, and here is why. There is a massive jump from thirty leads a week to 100 leads a week. When you needed thirty leads a week, you were spending a lot more time working in the business. Now you are not, you can increase your hours of marketing from ten to twenty hours a week, so double the time on lead generation can give you more than double the leads. You also have more people in your business and a larger network to build through.

When you look at the high number of consults versus the really low conversion of actual clients, this is for two reasons. 1) We have no idea what conversion or show rates your trainers will have. We cannot control this; at best we can influence it. 2) At this stage of our business we still want to be solely responsible for the sales target, which is four new clients a week, so it's your job to get that. Anything that the team sells is a bonus, and this guarantees our success through hedging.

At this stage, you may be thinking, how the heck do I generate 100 leads a week? There's no other way to tell you this, other than—you simply need a coach. We can show you how to generate 100-500 leads a week for minimal money. It's also impossible to share all forty-eight of our marketing strategies face-to-face and eighty online strategies in this book. I have done everything I can to give you a blueprint, and offered a ton of value with the space we have within this book.

3b) At this point, you have yourself and three other trainers delivering PT and semi-private.

This is where we now hire another two PTs, and appoint a head trainer or manager. We now have five trainers in the business plus yourself selling. Here are the targets to stay on track.

Generate 100 leads
Book 50 consults
Deliver 30 consults
Gain 6 new clients.

At this point the conversion rates of your early trainers will begin to increase, and your database is also increasing, so you are receiving more referrals and consults from internal marketing, which are better quality leads.

This is the point in the business when you need to review your venue. Is the venue you are at sufficient to have a big enough team to generate seven figures? If not, it's time to start looking. This may even come up early on, but it is something there needs to be a solution for as soon as possible.

3c) There are six of you in the business and now you hire two more trainers. One will be a manager. This gives you a team of eight total. A team of a minimum of eight is required for this model. Again, you don't have to use this model, and there are a variety of alternative ways you will reach your 7-figure business. I've simply outlined the fastest.

It's also important to note here that we approach the growth of the team the same as we do the growth of clients. If we lose a client in a week, and our target is two new clients that week in order to hit our target, we must gain three new clients to make up for the loss. The same goes with hiring trainers. If our target is two new trainers and we lose one, we need to bring on three next time, or in-between, hire another to make up for it. Make sense?

Here is a video outlining the steps to build a 7-figure fitness business in 12 months → https://youtu.be/gE0y0ofE72E

9

MONEY MASTERY FOR FITNESS BUSINESS OWNERS

When I first became qualified as a Personal Trainer in my early twenties, I had one thing on my mind. Get clients, get booked solid and train them. The last thing on my mind was paying taxes, nor did anyone teach me how it worked. I was hungry, but naïve and uneducated.

After several years of making a 6-figure income as a PT, one of my clients mentioned to me that I needed to pay taxes. Having no idea what my obligations were, I decided to go and see an accountant. All I remember is him shaking his head and saying, what a mess.

For years I had not tracked my finances, kept them organized, done any reports or paid any taxes. After weeks of work it was established I owed the Taxation Office more than $30,000 cash. And due to the overdue nature of the reports and payments, the Australian Tax Office gave me fourteen days to come up with the money or I would be forced into bankruptcy.

I was great at making money but was even better at spending it. I had zero savings and no way to raise the money. Luckily for me at the time, I was dating a girl who loaned me the money and I avoided bankruptcy.

One of the biggest mistakes I see personal trainers and business owners in general make is not putting aside tax, tracking their finances and keeping reports up to date. After working with literally thousands of PTs I know for a fact, there is a good chance as you read this, it may be you. Imagine building a successful business where all your bills are paid, all your taxes are paid on time, you have zero bad debt and actually have money left over every week.

As I write this, this book is literally ready to be sent to the publishers, the cover has even been designed. But as I took one last look through this book, I asked myself, what was missing?

See, this book is written for hungry and ambitious trainers that want a real business. That want more from life. That don't just simply want to be booked solid for years then burn out. But if you can't get your finances and affairs straight, that will never happen. And it will create more stress than is necessary.

So, in this chapter, not only will I cover the four reports all business owners use to build a big business, but also, you are going to be making more money than you need, so the question is: what do you do with this money?

In this chapter, using my personal financial freedom philosophy, I will guide you to creating a system that allows you to stop living week to week, create financial freedom and even become a millionaire.

I have a millionaire's inner circle program where I teach people how to become a millionaire within three years. It's very exclusive and invite only. But the information in this chapter is the financial foundational philosophy we use in this program. And If you choose to use it too, you can take as many holidays as you desire, build a property portfolio and even a gym or other investment business portfolio.

Regardless of your level of ambition, it's no secret that building a big business is easier than keeping it. If you apply the financial strategies in this chapter, you too can master the money game as a fitness business owner, and if you stay the course, even become a millionaire.

THE FINANCIAL TRACKING SYSTEM OF MILLIONAIRES

There are four main reports that all true business owners understand, read, and keep up to date:

1. Budget
2. Cash flow projections
3. Balance sheet
4. Profit and loss statement.

In this section I will share a basic strategy for each.

BUDGETING

Why Have a Budget?

Your budget is your financial map to increasing your efficiency in cash flow management. It guarantees that debtors and business expenses are paid on time, all tax obligations are met, and it helps increase your income.

What is Budgeting?

Budgeting is a means of expressing your business goals in financial or monetary terms. Budgets can be prepared for sales, expenses, purchases, cash flow, and production. Although budgeting is considered to be an essential tool for all businesses, it is sometimes said that a small business need not be as disciplined as a big business in this area of financial management; it is due to this limiting belief that a small business fails to grow into a big business. Budgets are management tools, and must be considered as vital components to the success of your business. Budgeting increases your decision-making ability by providing comparative performance indicators.

Having decided to prepare a set of budgets, it becomes an element of your overall business plan, and therefore it should be constantly referred to, modified if necessary, but above all used as a financial reference point that indicates to you, the business owner, how you are proceeding financially at any point in time. Having prepared a budget projection and established a comparison to actual performance, the final task in the management control process is to analyze the variances and understand why the variances occurred.

WORK OUT A REALISTIC BUDGET

Once you have completed your realistic budget, you may find you are still spending more than you earn. You have two choices. You could frugally change your lifestyle, or increase your income—doing both is even better! Your budget is a document that tells you what your expenses are and what your capacity to save is.

To complete your budget, simply add all your expenses in the required row for that item for the next twelve weeks. Just like the projections, you want to update it weekly, add any new expenses, and create a new page at the beginning of every month.

Budget 2018					
		April			
Expenses	2-8th	9-15th	16-22nd	23-29th	Total
BAS					$-
Income Tax					$-
Rent					$-
Food					$-
Car					$-
Savings					$-
Charity					$-
Property account					$-
Investing account					$-
Travel					$-
Outsourcing					$-
Trainer 1					$-
Trainer 2					$-
Gym Rent					
Click funnels					$-
Skype					$-
Zoom					$-
Site5					$-
Phone					$-
Cleaner					
Insurance					$-
Fiverr					$-
Facebook					$-
Supplements					
Accountant/Legal					$-
Total Expenses	$-	$-	$-	$-	$-
Income					

FINANCIAL PROJECTIONS

Imagine if you knew exactly how much you were going to earn each week for the next twelve weeks. It would allow you to budget for things like birthdays, Xmas and holidays, and give you more clarity and certainty about where you are heading and what you need to do to improve. On this spreadsheet, you will find a column to write the names of all of your active clients on direct debit only (as they are your only sure client payments) from your database, then simply add in each column how much you make from them. Example: if they do one session each week it is $25; if two it is $50; or if they are a partnered doing one session each week it will be $18.75 for one or $37.50 for two.

Be sure to add group sessions you are planning on doing by adding GT in the left panel and $60 for each class. It is important to always have the next twelve weeks available, so at the beginning of each month, create a new page to be able to see the next twelve weeks. You may keep old records to check on progress. Make sure you add any new clients as soon as you sign them up, and update this weekly. I recommend doing all your spreadsheets together or in two sections: Monday morning client tracking, and Monday afternoon, financial tracking.

	2018 Projections				
		March			
	Name	12-18th	19-25th	26-1st	Total
	PT				
1	Tom Bellows	$99.00	$99.00	$99.00	**$297.00**
2	Sarah Smith	$99.00	$99.00	$99.00	**$297.00**
3	Anthony Peters	$99.00	$99.00	$99.00	**$297.00**
4	Richard Alan	$49.00	$49.00	$49.00	**$147.00**
5	Tabitha shine	$49.00	$49.00	$49.00	**$147.00**
6	Liam Tricky	$49.00	$49.00	$49.00	**$147.00**
7					
8					
9					
10					
	10				
	0	**$444.00**	**$444.00**	**$444.00**	**$1,332.00**

PROFIT AND LOSS STATEMENT

The two main financial reports prepared by all types of businesses are: statement of financial performance (profit and loss Statement); statement of financial position (balance sheet).

The format of these reports will vary from business to business and the reporting requirement required by the business owner(s) or the law. However, all financial reports revolve around five types of business classifications. These classifications are: assets, liabilities, owner's equity, revenues, expenses.

Assets are items of value owned by the business and things that attract money into the business. Assets are usually purchased to assist in producing revenue; for example, property, equipment, investments, buildings; or they result from trading, such as debtors (accounts receivable), stock (inventory), and cash in the bank or petty cash. You should remember that if the business is acquiring an item of value, that will add value to the business, or money is owed to it; then the item should be classified as an asset.

Liabilities: these are amounts of money owed by the business to others. Examples include creditors, accounts payable, bank overdraft, GST payable, mortgage, and loans payable to the business.

Owner's equity: this is the owner's investment in the business. The accounts that make up this classification are capital (when the owner puts money or assets into the business) and drawings (when money or assets are taken from the business by the owner).

Revenues: revenues are items of income earned by the business as a result of engaging in activities designed to derive a profit. Examples include sales (of services), interest received (on investments), commissions received, discounts received, and dividends received (on investments).

Expenses: expenses can be defined as the costs of operating the business on a daily basis. Examples include: rent, rates, stationery, advertising, motor vehicle expenses, purchase expenses, and freight on goods. The list of expenses can be extensive. You should remember that if money is being spent on an item that is not adding value to the business as an asset does, or the item was not a liability (owing), it will most likely be an expense.

Business Name
Address 1
Address 2

Profit & Loss Statement

July 2017 through June 2018

	July	August	September	Total
Income				$0.00
PT Income				$0.00
Bootcamp Income				$0.00
Online				$0.00
Other				$0.00
Total Income				$0.00
Expenses				
Business expenses				$0.00
Rent				$0.00
Car				$0.00
Equipment				$0.00
Education & training				$0.00
Uniform				$0.00
Stationery				$0.00
Internet and telecommunications				$0.00
Computer & electrical				$0.00
Total expenses				$0.00
Gross profit	$0.00	$0.00	$0.00	$0.00
Personal drawings				$-

BALANCE SHEET

A balance sheet is basically a list of your assets and liabilities. Your assets are things that put money into your bank account, and liabilities are things that take money out of your bank account. This is one of the most important, if not *the* most important sheet you will ever use in finances.

In the beginning, most people have debt and minimal assets, so I have created a unique version of a balance sheet. In our business, wealth and life coaching programs, we assist people in creating and using all four of these financial tracking sheets. On the next page, I have shown the basic yet powerful sheet we use to assist people to get out of debt, save money, create financial freedom, invest, then build wealth.

I highly recommend you do the same!

Balance Sheet						
Targets		**March**				
	Total Target	26-4th	5-11th	12-18th	19-25th	26-1st
DD income						
Bank transfers						
MLM income						
CF income						
Coaching						
Stripe						
TOTAL INCOME	$-	$-	$-	$-	$-	$-
Credit card						
Loan						
Car						
Total Debt	$-	$-	$-	$-	$-	$-
Business account						
Everyday account						
Savings account						
GST offset account						
Travel account						
Property account						
Business investing account						
TOTAL SAVINGS	$-	$-	$-	$-	$-	$-
Net Worth						

CREATING YOUR FINANCIAL FREEDOM ACCOUNTS

If you speak to almost anyone who has achieved any significant level of financial success, you might be surprised to find out that they in fact use many bank accounts. Why would they do this? Several reasons. Firstly, they usually have multiple income streams, and secondly, so they can have awareness of what exactly is happening with the different income streams. If you had three businesses, would you not have three business bank accounts? And if you had three businesses, how many tax returns would you need to do? Three, right? So, you want to do the same for your bank accounts. Of course, mainly for accounting purposes, but also because you can have clarity on what is going where. Imagine if you knew exactly how much you were going to earn each week for the next twelve weeks, would that allow you to sleep better at night? What about if you knew your exact expenses for the next twelve weeks then stuck to them? By having multiple bank accounts, we can clearly create an individual plan for all the financial aspects of our economic life.

Here is the financial philosophy we personally use and share with thousands—how to stop living week-to-week and create financial freedom. If you choose to action this plan completely, you too will stop living week-to-week within the next four weeks. How badly do you want it? Many people will read this and not action it, while some will read this and create the plan and set up the accounts, but never create the habit and follow through. Some people, the special ones committed to a dream lifestyle, will stick to this philosophy 100% and create their dream lifestyle. Who will you be?

Included below are the seven bank accounts we strongly suggest you set up today. It's important to understand it's not just the amounts, or percentages, as we understand it can change for everyone. What is important is that you go out today, create the bank accounts and start habituating your financial freedom plan.

Here is an outline of the seven bank accounts and how to use them. **The following scenario below is for a small business owner.**

Bank Account 1: Business Account 20-40% of your gross Income
If you don't yet have a business of some description, it will be very difficult to create financial freedom. If you follow the steps, you too can create financial freedom.

If you do have a business already, using this financial philosophy, I suggest using no more than twenty percent of the business's gross income for business expenses. I understand there are many different business models, and you may even have a company. The same principle applies whether you have one business, three businesses or a company. It's twenty percent total of all the businesses or company combined. If you have a business with staff or contractors, I understand expenses can be higher, even much higher. If that is the case you will probably also have more cash flow. So, although the percentage of business expenses may be higher, your total cash flow after expenses will also be higher. This is a starting point and a recommendation.

If you don't yet have a business, you will find in fact it will usually be much lower than twenty percent. However, if you have a registered company and perhaps sell products, it may be much higher.

I have been asked many times about using a business credit card. If you are serious about creating financial freedom, which I'm guessing you are or you wouldn't be reading this, my recommendation is to cut up your credit card right now. Why do you need it? Why have a resource that, when you are already struggling or not living financially the way you want, can hold you back and get you in more debt? You can use a debit card instead. You will avoid temptation and not get yourself in more debt. A debit card allows you to order and book things over the phone or online if you need to, and can be used as a credit card. If you truly desire financial freedom and are still living week-to-week, pull out that credit card right now and cut it in half; it's only doing you more damage. If you are reading this going, no way will I cut up my credit card, that's who I normally find out has the most debt or money owing. Yes, it might help your credit rating short-term, but the more money owing on your credit card, the lower your borrowing capacity to increase your net worth, and the more bad debt you can get into.

Bank Account 2: Everyday Account 20-40% of your Income
To truly get ahead financially we really want to become frugal in our daily spending. Cigarettes, alcohol and fast food are a good start to eliminating waste. Buying unnecessary items like clothing, music,

movies, games and other low-cost items are a great way to get stuck in the rat race of living week-to-week.

The second bank account you want is one you probably already have, but how do you use it? The second bank account is an everyday savings account. Again, if you have a credit card linked to your everyday account, I would cut it up immediately and replace it with a debit card. If you are a business owner (or when you are a business owner), each week you will transfer twenty to forty percent of your gross income into an everyday savings account and use it for your living expenses. Utilities, mortgage, rent, food, and necessities. We start by living within our means first, then create more cash flow and *then* increase our level and standard of living. Many have it the other way around. This is also a good time to create a budget and begin to stick to it.

If you are not yet a business owner, then this percentage will probably be higher, for the simple fact that your income is probably lower and taxes are paid by your employer. In the case of an employee, I would suggest using sixty percent of your total income for your everyday account.

Again, I understand that this varies a lot depending on your total income; however, it's important to remember that it's more about creating the habit of frugality here (spending more wisely and not spending more than your budget).

If you do own a large business or company, the above percentages may be quite different. However, as stated above, the purpose of this philosophy is to follow it and create the bank accounts. Especially the bank accounts below. Simply work out your own numbers or percentages, as this is simply a guide. I believe most people who read this won't actually own a business, or if they do it will be a small business doing under seven figures a year.

Bank Account 3: Long-Term Savings 10% of your income

Next, we have the long-term savings account. You know the one we all know we should have but don't? Or we do have it but are not disciplined with it. I say, throw discipline out the window. Instead, do as I did when I was younger, when I would waste so much money. I set up an automated direct debit with my bank, so every Friday the bank would automatically deduct a sum of money from my business account and transfer it into my long-term savings account. I would also hide that account on my net bank (online banking) so I couldn't even see the account online. Out of sight, out of mind. I call this the law of positioning. Position yourself in a way so that you cannot fail. I'm usually pretty disciplined when I've made a choice to create a habit. But if I come home after a long day and I'm hungry, I walk to the fridge and open the fridge door, and staring back at me is an open packet of M&M's, and I look over my shoulder and no one is there, I'm going to reach in and grab a handful of that delicious chocolaty goodness. Then I would probably do what most do, and eat the whole packet. It's really simple, if you don't want to eat the chocolate, why tempt fate, don't buy the chocolate in the first place or have it in the fridge.

This bank account I believe is the easiest and simplest to set up, but usually the first step for most people when creating financial freedom. Habituating not just saving, but spending less than you earn, is vital to your success. If you take nothing else from this entire philosophy, and just apply this one thing, you will stop living week-to-week within the next four weeks.

Finally, you may be thinking, 'well Jason this is great, but I only earn around $500, $300 or even less than that a week'. Again, this is not just about the percentages, it's about creating the habit. It's not how much you save, it's that you just save religiously! I was doing a live presentation on this philosophy recently, and a young lady announced that she was making less than $500 a week, and there was no way she could put aside ten percent of savings after living expenses. I replied, 'That's great, because that's exactly what this financial freedom plan will help you do.'

I asked her, 'Could you, this week open the account and deposit just $1 into the account?' Of course, she replied with, 'Yes!' Then I continued to ask if the following week she could deposit $2, then the following $4, then the following week (week four) $8. And of course, she replied, 'yes'. I had her set up that account, then explained that gives us four weeks to implement the rest of the financial freedom plan, start making residual income, and increase your cash flow. When we get to the five-, six-, seven-, eight-, nine- and ten-week mark, you will be ahead financially.

So you see, it's not just about the percentage, it's about creating the habit. Get up right now, go to the bank or login to your bank online, and set up this bank account. Organize a regular automated debit, and stop living week-to-week today.

Bank Account 4: GST Offset Account/Tax Account 10-20% of your gross income
Firstly, I will start by saying I am not a CPA or a qualified accountant. Always follow what your accountant suggests (after doing your due diligence, of course, in choosing an accountant)!

When you are a business owner, you will need to set up a fourth bank account. The fourth account is to put aside your tax regularly in advance. Depending on your business cash cycle, it will usually be weekly or monthly—the frequency at which your business is paid. The income stream resources in this book will pay you weekly or monthly. For example, a personal training business owner could get paid daily, but they set up a direct debit system where they are paid in one lump sum, weekly. Therefore, you would put your tax aside every week so you don't stress when the taxman comes to you wanting money. A GST offset account in Australia is an account that attracts high interest, and an account you can withdraw from frequently without it negatively impacting your accrued interest. Most countries have a similar account, so be sure to talk to your accountant and bookkeeper (if you don't have one, now is a good time to get one) to organize your taxes effectively in advance.

Try not to become a man of success but rather try to become a man of value.

~ Albert Einstein

Bank Account 5: Investment Account 10% of your income
Although you may or may not yet know how to invest or what to invest in, if you are reading this book, I know you are hungry and you are ambitious. Therefor you also understand that cash flow is king for sure; however, the next step is to invest and build net worth.

We do that through investing and building a property portfolio, business portfolio, and share portfolio.

Every week I personally put money into accounts on autopilot for my next investment gym/business, my next investment property, and shares (stocks outside of Australia).

The better you get at this the more wealth you will create.

Set up an investment bank account today and start saving for your next property as you learn how to invest!

Bank Account 6: Travel Account 10% of your income
This is where the fun begins.

How do we create the financial leverage and cash flow to enable you to afford all of those magical experiences? We do this with the sixth bank account; the travel account. Many people who struggle with money will say things like: 'I can't afford it!' or 'when I can afford it!' These are both legitimate statements if you have a poor mindset. Someone with a financially free mindset would ask a question such as: *'how* can I afford it?'

Instead of living life in reaction and by default, you will begin to choose what you want, then set a plan for its attainment.

As you journey through this paradigm shift to a financially free mindset, you will discover that beyond a maze of fear, doubt and uncertainty, the only real thing that was stopping you was you. You will begin to feel more confident, and make choices based on what you want in your life, not what you believe has been served to you. It will empower you with a sense of control and certainty unlike ever before. You will feel more motivated to take action every day, and do whatever it takes, because you realize you can actually achieve anything you put your mind to.

To fuel the financial fire necessary for your travel, the first thing you want to do is set up your sixth bank account—your travel account. Once you have your account set up and know your weekly or monthly target that you need to save, as calculated in the travel plan section, we need to get you making some extra money. If I were to say to you that if you were to work for just ten to twenty hours a week (part-time) for the next three to five years, you would never have to work again, would you be prepared to do it? Of course, right?

We have helped endless numbers of people to make an extra $1000-$2000 a month residual income in just the first twelve weeks. That's a minimum of $12,000 a year for travel. How would you like an extra $12,000 a year for travelling in the next three months?

WHAT NOW?

This chapter may be the most important for your financial future. I truly hope you take the time to create these four financial tracking sheets, set up your automatic accounts, and start building your wealth. Cut up your credit card right now, set up your bank accounts, and put them on autopilot.

Bonus Chapter I
BUILD A SUCCESSFUL BOOTCAMP BUSINESS

There's no doubt that one-on-one Personal Training is the bread and butter of Personal Trainers. But once we are booked solid, or as we look for leverage of time and increase of profit margins, Personal Trainers often turn their focus to bootcamp.

It's easy to do it on a shoestring and for next to zero cost. It can also be done almost anywhere (depending on your local council).

The seduction of bootcamp is in the potential earning capacity per hour. If I charge $50 for 30 minute PT sessions, then I make $100 an hour. BUT… If I charge $20 for bootcamp for an hour and have 20 members, I now make $400; that is a 400% increase in income for the same time.

What we fail to recognize though, is that to accomplish this, the numbers in our marketing funnel are drastically different. What do I mean by this?

For example, let's say I have a 50% conversion rate. To gain one new PT client, I would need to deliver 2 free consults and book 4 free consults. To get 4 booked consults I would need to generate 8 leads.

So, to build to 6 figures with PT, here are my numbers:

1. Generate 160 leads
2. Book 80 consults
3. Deliver 40 showed consults
4. Gain 20 clients doing 2 sessions each week at $50

   = $2000 a week.

Let's look at the numbers to build a 6-figure bootcamp business.

If I charge $10 a session, and each member does 3 a week = $30 a week per member, here are the numbers to build a 6-figure Bootcamp at the same conversion rates:

1. Generate 528 leads
2. Book 264 free consults or trials
3. Do 132 consults or free trials
4. 66 members = $2000 a week (6 figures).

I understand these numbers are just an example, and definitely subject to change, and you probably have a higher conversion rate, especially of bootcamp to PT ratio. BUT the truth is, to make the same income total from bootcamp as PT, we need to do four times the amount of marketing and generate four times the amount of leads.

I'm definitely not saying don't do bootcamp. It's just important to be aware of the numbers.

Look back at your four options once booked solid:

1. Launch semi-private
2. Launch bootcamp
3. Hire a trainer
4. Launch online

Another challenge with a bootcamp, especially if you are in a gym, is that it can take you away from where you are building your current business and where you make most of your money, not to mention the travel time involved. Imagine if you thought like a real business owner and hired someone else to build your bootcamp!

It's also a little slower to build a bootcamp than to build another PT with one-on-one or semi-private, BUT definitely faster than building online—well at least for the first few months.

Now we have looked at some of the challenges of bootcamp, let's look at some of the advantages. For I do still believe you want to have bootcamp in your value ladder for your large fitness business.

Bootcamp is an amazing platform to build a real community. A place where people feel they are a part of something greater than themselves. A place where people can socialize, meet new people and get their hit of oxytocin!

Personally, I believe bootcamp definitely has a place in a fitness business, because, in the value ladder in this book, we want to create a complete ecosystem. And each service is a link in the chain to provide more and more value, and take each client on a journey that requires and desires more attention and results.

There is no denying one-on-one PT will give a client greater results but the fact is some people just won't be interested in PT.

As discussed in the earlier chapter, I truly believe bootcamp as a primary stream of income is dead. If you are relying on bootcamp to pay your bills, I believe you will struggle in the future. Bootcamp in a real fitness business, and community and ecosystem are crucial components. However, if you understand the sales funnel explained in the earlier chapter you will truly understand what all the large corporations of this world understand: that bootcamp is a front-end product., We use bootcamp to funnel people into our community and business, and then upsell them PT, Semi-private, workshops, challenges etcetera.

If you utilize your bootcamp in this fashion you will crush it! Gyms do the same; they offer a free pass to get in front of more people, upsell them the lowest, cheapest option, then upsell the high-ticket service, say one-on-one PT!

In this chapter, I'm going to give you an exact step-by-step plan on how you can build a 6-figure bootcamp in just 90 days.

Yes, you read that right. How to structure, market, launch, then deliver it. I have set up literally hundreds of bootcamp businesses all across the globe, and the way I'm going to show you is the fastest way to book your bootcamps solid. If you are coachable, trust in the system, and follow this 100%, your bootcamp alone will generate $2000 a week PLUS within next 3-6 months.

Imagine that…

Step 1) Your Model and Sales System

The first step is to create your product. As you know from the previous chapters, I'm a huge fan of showing potential clients the visual aid with payment options on a PowerPoint with your iPad or tablet. It simply looks professional, it's cutting edge, and it's something tangible they can see and touch, making it more real and credible.

As with personal training, start by creating a checklist of what your members will receive when they sign up. I never sell time, I always sell results. I sell results via a membership, package or subscription to increase perceived value and justify charging top dollar.

You can see an example below of the PowerPoint template we use with coaching clients.

Use the template as an example and create your own version. I'm sure you can do a better job and make it more visually appealing.

Here is an example of the PowerPoint package presentation:

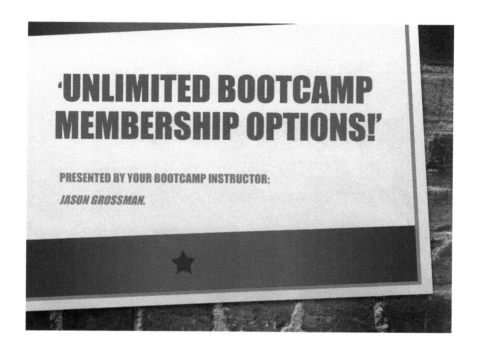

THE MEMBERSHIP INCLUDES

- UNLIMITED ACCESS TO OUR ENTIRE BOOTCAMP TIMETABLE
- 2 X FREE PERSONAL TRAINING SESSIONS
- ACCESS TO OUT FACEBOOK VIP GROUP
- ACCESS TO OUR EMAIL NEWSLETTER
- 2 X FREE 7 DAY GUEST PASSES FOR A FRIEND
- ACCESS TO OUR REGULAR SOCIAL EVENTS
- FITNESS AND NUTRITION TIPS

The membership should include at least 8-12 bullet points for increased perceived value.

It's also important to note all new members get two free PT sessions, so you have a chance to upsell them on PT as well. If we book their first free PT session on point of sale, we can strike while the iron is hot and they are excited about their new journey. I NEVER suggest combining services; I always keep them separate in my value ladder and sales funnels. This makes it more streamlined, easier to track, and maintains consistency of clients' payments within the business. Not to mention it maximizes profits.

So anyone who pays for bootcamp and PT will pay the same price and full price for each one.

Once you have created your checklist using the above example, it's important to determine your price. The price on the above template is in Australian Dollars (AUD). This is the minimum price I would suggest. If you are in the United States this is also the lowest price.

If you are in the United Kingdom, I would suggest no less than 15 pounds a week and 20 pounds.

Side Note: I understand in the UK most people get paid monthly, so you can offer a monthly option.

You will notice in the above template that the payment options are a double bind. An A or B option. This removes the notion of the choice of giving a no answer when asking for the sale. If I ask a question that can lead to a no answer, seventy-five percent of the time I will get a no.

Notice the difference:

'Do you want to start training with me?'

Versus:

'When do you want to start training with me?'

The first question gives you the option to say no, the second doesn't.

I strongly suggest using the double bind option to sell your bootcamp of a 3 months membership at $49 unlimited access to timetable, or $39 a week for 6 Months.

This gives them a false sense of choice. They feel they can choose the price they wish to pay OR the length of time. This de-frames the two biggest objections in sales—time and money.

To make bootcamp work with our system, you need at least three sessions a week to justify the unlimited membership option. We will cover this in this chapter and show you how to launch three sessions and book them solid in just weeks!

Take the time now to do your checklist, create your PowerPoint, and determine your prices.

As with all services, this will be direct debit. I NEVER take cash or upfront, because then I cannot forecast my income or budget effectively. I also then have inconsistent income, and wouldn't you rather a consistent income? Wouldn't you rather an income you can control?

OTHER TOOLS

Other tools you will need, of course, include: the pre-exercise questionnaire that all new members will fill out before their first session; terms and conditions when they sign up; and direct debit forms. You should have all these tools from the earlier PT sales chapter.

7-DAY GUEST PASS SYSTEM

Once you have all your tools we need to create your sales system. After eighteen years in this industry as I write this book, and building hundreds of bootcamp businesses, I have experimented with almost every model and sales system you can imagine. The system I'm about to share with you I truly believe to be the fastest and most efficient system in the world.

Step 1) Create a 7-Day Guest Pass
You want to create a voucher for a free 7-day guest pass. I suggest using a business card backing. Have one side your actual business card, and the other side a 7-day guest pass to your bootcamp timetable. I understand you will probably already have a two free PT session vouchers also. So, you will have some business cards that will have two free PT sessions on the back and some with 7-day guest pass. I would suggest ordering 250-500 of each to start with!

Be sure to make it matt, NOT glossy, so you can write the date thirty days from now as the expiry date. You want your voucher to have exclusivity, time sensitivity, and increased perceived value. So, having expiry, dollar value, and handing them out only when people earn or deserve them will accomplish this. When done correctly your vouchers can become like currency!

Step 2) Booking Leads
Once you have your vouchers and you are generating leads (we will cover that in a moment) you can contact the lead to book them AND

a friend to come and collect their 7-day guest pass. That's the great thing about generating these leads. Every lead doubles, because you always promote it as you and a friend. Whenever you generate a lead and book them in, you always have them bring someone, as this increases your show rate and doubles your sales potential.

Step 3) Collecting the 7-day pass

When they come and collect the gift voucher with a friend, you meet with them before the bootcamp session so they can fill out the pre-exercise questionnaire, and then physically hand them the 7-day pass with the expiry date. You then only hand out the voucher in exchange for a booking 7 days from now. Which means in 7 days from now, you will meet with them after their last free Bootcamp sessions.

Step 4) Closing the sale

At the end of their last free session (7 days from receiving their voucher) you will show them your bootcamp PowerPoint presentation above, sign them on the direct debit form or system, then fill out two terms and conditions. They get one and you get the other.

As soon as you complete the forms you say this: 'As a part of the bootcamp membership you are entitled to two free personal training sessions, so let's book them now. Is morning or afternoon easier for you next week? You book them in with a PT, and then that PT will upsell them personal training and continue to take the client through the value ladder to better service them, plug them into their community, and give them greater results.

THE 3 RULES OF A 7-DAY GUEST PASS

Rather than diminishing the quality of your vouchers, there is a way to actually have them perceived as currency. Here is how.

Rule 1) Always hand out two vouchers. Never less, never more. For you and a friend. This will double our lead generation efforts for the same amount of work.

Rule 2) Only hand out vouchers to non-paying clients in exchange for an appointment. This appointment of course is to upsell them bootcamp.

Rule 3) Only hand out vouchers to paying clients in exchange for a contact number. This activates the voucher, and you can write their name and expiry, making it more personal.

You can watch the full video of how to build a 6-figure bootcamp in Just 90 Days on YouTube here → https://youtu.be/hJ1QP4PyOc0

Guest Pass Example:

MARKETING YOUR NEW BOOTCAMP

OK, so you decide to launch a bootcamp, or you already do bootcamp but it's not really growing. After eighteen years in the industry and fifteen years of building bootcamps, here is the BEST launch process I have ever seen. In fact, when it is done correctly, you will book three to five bootcamps a week solid in just weeks:

Step 1) Determine a date/week for your launch week. We will promote it as a launch week as something new. Even if you have an existing bootcamp business, you will still use the same process. You will need three weeks to market it effectively. So, it will be three-and-a-half to four weeks away, minimum Monday–Saturday or Tuesday–Sunday.

Then determine what times your three launch bootcamps will be on. My suggestion is Tuesday, Wednesday or Thursday evening, somewhere between 6.30–8 p.m. These will get more numbers generally than others. Early mornings can work also, but it depends on weather and location more. Say 6 a.m. And of course, you have the option of Saturday early or mid-morning. I have found Saturday gets more registered but also gets more cancellations. At the end of the day, I don't have a crystal ball and know which times will be best for you, so start with these familiar times and test and work it out for yourself. But this should be a good starting point.

Personally, I like one hour but you could also do forty-five minutes. Remember you need time to set up, have new clients fill out forms, then huddle and upsell, then pack up after session.

Step 2) Follow this three-week marketing plan to book solid your bootcamps.

The first three bootcamps will be free to bring in as many numbers as possible, then you can upsell our services. It's essentially one big 7-day guest pass.

Here is the exact three-week marketing campaign we use to launch a new bootcamp:

1) Create a free account at http://eventbrite.com or another free event site. You could also create a click funnel page. This allows you to capture people's contact details online.

2) Create event with description on Eventbrite. Once you set up the event, you will need to go to 'manage event', then click on order form on the left and be sure to tick the two boxes, so that way you are

getting everyone's phone number, or you cannot ring and confirm!

3) Create a Facebook event with link to Eventbrite for online registration through your personal profile, and one each for your groups. If you have more than 500 friends, you may need to create more than one event.

Simply copy the details from your Eventbrite event and paste them into your Facebook event, AND add the link to your Eventbrite registration page.

4) Post on your personal wall a link to your Facebook event, and tag all your clients so their friends see it through their newsfeed. Also post in every group and page you have.

You will post twice a day in each Facebook event. A social proof and an add value post. Client testimonials, results, videos, images. Also, articles, blogs, videos, info graphics etcetera.

5) Create a free www.mailchimp.com email marketing account or other account, create a list for your entire database, and copy EVERY email address you have in there. Then send a bulk email with a link to your Eventbrite event each week for three weeks. I suggest every Monday. We currently use Send Grid Via Click funnels.

6) Download ExcelSMS (otherwise known as SA Group Text) from iPhone or android or another bulk text app, and send a bulk text to everyone you have a phone number for with a link to Eventbrite each week for three weeks. I suggest every Monday.

7) Have all your attendees on the Facebook event, your friends, clients, family, and partner invite all their friends (send them a Facebook message asking them and also who they will be bringing). You can offer an incentive, a free PT session, something else or even an extra ticket to enter the prize draw.

8) Get yourself a clipboard and piece of paper made up on an excel spreadsheet then printed. Include name and number at the top. Place it on the clipboard. Then you are going to register ALL of your PT

Clients AND one friend on that clipboard, then they will go home and enter their details on the Eventbrite themselves. This gives you control so you are not just relying on them visiting the registration page. ALSO, be sure to register anyone else you come into face-to-face contact with. If you have PTs working for you, give them a clipboard each.

9) Repeat email/text/ blast three weeks in a row and Facebook and clipboard daily!

10) The MOST Important part now is to RING EVERYONE the day before and confirm they are coming, and the magical question—who are they bringing. This gives you another opportunity for a boost in numbers the day before and locks them in. I even like to text them AS WELL the same day.

LAUNCHING YOUR BOOTCAMP

For your launch week, the most Important part is to ring everyone the day before the booking and then ask who else they wish to bring. Beyond that, how can you make it memorable? Do you have a fruit platter, champagne toast? Do you do a social event afterwards with rock climbing or ten pin bowling? Do you have a theme with games and prizes?

Be creative and innovative and do things so they will remember and talk about for years to come!

THE HUDDLE

Something that I believe is super-important is how you finish each bootcamp. I use a process called the huddle. At the end of EVERY bootcamp session, we bring everyone together in a circle. I ask three to four yes sets, that is, questions that lead to a yes answer. They call out loud and it leaves them on a high! For example, who enjoyed today? And I raise my hand...

After the yes sets, I announce the importance of booking in for the next bootcamp, so we pass a clipboard around (a little archaic I know but effective) and everyone writes their details down to register for the next session. I also ask them who is not here today whom you know who would love this. Be sure to bring them next time. Or come and see me and I will give you a free guest pass to give to them.

Then before we finish, I make any announcements and get a group photo, which we post every time on Facebook and tag everyone for their friends to see.

Finally, after the huddle, I simply ask those who are at the end of their free seven-day pass, please stay behind and come and see me.

Now I'm with just the people I need to sign up, I can whip out my iPad or tablet, show them my PowerPoint package, sign them up, and book them for their free PT sessions.

If you habituate this process you will crush it, and it will rain down on you hard with referrals unlike anything you have ever seen!

After you launch and you book your sessions solid, only add one session at a time to your timetable to keep it consolidated and maximize numbers. Keep building, then hire trainers to your desired size!

Setting up lead boxes for local businesses and online strategies is also very powerful for bootcamp; these strategies are covered in other chapters of this book.

FREE VIDEO:

To watch the FREE comprehensive video on YouTube on this entire process and how to build a 6-figure bootcamp in just 90 days, simply visit our YouTube Channel or this direct link

→ https://youtu.be/hJ1QP4PyOc0

Bonus Chapter II

BUILD A SUCCESSFUL SEMI-PRIVATE BUSINESS

Personally, I believe semi-private personal training is the most underused and most undervalued service in a PT's arsenal.

But what is semi-private? I guess different experts will have slightly different opinions or definitions, but for me, it's delivering a VIP service to up to four individuals at a time. It's still exclusive but not one-on-one.

In this section, I'm going to share with you how to build a $5000 a week semi-private business. Yes, you read that right!

So why semi-private? A few reasons. Firstly, there are many people that simply want to train with a friend. Some people are looking for a more affordable option. Also, the profit margins are insane.

If you train someone for 30 minutes at $50 you make $100 an hour. But If you charge someone just $40 for a 45 minute session with 4 people you are now making $160 for 45 minutes, or $213 an hour. More than double the income for the same amount of work. Well essentially. The beauty with semi-private is you only need two clients plus their friends. So, to make the extra income per hour, you don't need to generate an insane amount of leads like you do with bootcamp.

When to use SP (semi-private)? I've found that once a trainer is booked solid, sometimes that trainer is not in a location to hire another PT, or simply doesn't wish to. If that is the case, how do you continue to build your business and increase your income once you are booked solid? I believe the best way, if you cannot or do not wish to hire a PT, is SP.

FREE LIVE VIDEO:

Here is a comprehensive video on the entire process
→ https://youtu.be/zIKrnzWLnu0

HOW TO CREATE YOUR SEMI-PRIVATE MODEL

Since we have already covered this in creating your PT & bootcamp packages, we don't need to spend much time on this. but as a guide, this is my suggestion. Whatever you charge for 30 minute PT sessions (this model won't work for one-hour sessions), for example $50, you will add 15 minutes but reduce charge by $10.

For example, if you charge $50 for 30 minutes one-on-one PT, then you would charge $40 for 45 minutes each person for semi-private. Here is why:

Once you are booked solid with PT, to continue to grow your business, you need to increase your leverage through people, time, money or resources. As you know, your main options are: 1) hire a PT; 2) launch online; 3) consolidate with bootcamp; or 4) consolidate with SP.

If you choose to launch SP, which I will show you how to do in this chapter, and book 10 sessions solid within 4 weeks, you could say to your current clients, how would you feel if I were to give you an extra 15 minutes with me in each session, AND also make the price

$10 less? Just $40 a session! What do you think most clients will say? Yes, right? So, you can start to funnel your PT clients into SP and even have some clients doing both. This frees up more time for you to help more people, have more clients, fit more people in at peak times, and so on.

Again, you don't have to deliver SP; I just think if you want a large fitness business you want a completed value ladder with all of these services sooner or later. And the profit margins are incredibly high!

HOW TO LAUNCH YOUR SEMI-PRIVATE SERVICE OR BUSINESS

It's similar to launching your bootcamp; however, instead of locking in 3 time slots, you are going to determine 10 x 45 minute time slots to do a 3-week marketing campaign for and book them solid.

My suggestion is to have 3-4 in each of the 3 peak times. Early mornings 5-7 a. m., crêche/mums' time 9–11 a.m, and evenings 6–8 p.m. Why? I understand you already have clients in these times, BUT by opening up an SP session in each of these times, you can now service more people in the busy times, make more money, and impact more lives. Also, unlike bootcamp, you don't need to leave the gym or your place of business to deliver the sessions.

Once you have determined your 10 time slots, it may look like this:

1. *Monday 7.30–8.1 5 p.m.*
2. *Tuesday 6–6.45 a.m.*
3. *Tuesday 7.30–8.15 p.m.*
4. *Wednesday 6–6.45 a.m.*
5. *Wednesday 9.30–10.15 a.m.*
6. *Thursday 6–6.45 a.m.*
7. *Thursday 7.30–8.15 p.m.*
8. *Friday 6–6.45 a.m.*
9. *Friday 9.30–10.15 a.m.*
10. *Saturday 9–9.45 a.m.*

Now you want to create a spreadsheet to print and place on a clipboard. On that piece of paper, you will have each of the 10 time slots above with 6 available spaces, to book 6 people with their name and phone number. Why 6? Because our goal is to launch with 10 sessions booked solid. When we launch this free week of 10 SP sessions, we want 4 people to show up to all 10 sessions; by booking 6 people for each, even if 2 cancel or don't show, we still have 4 show up; make sense?

So, the goal is to use the three-week marketing campaign in the bootcamp chapter, and book sixty people onto that piece of paper for a FREE SP session. Each person can only attend one free session for the week, which means that is sixty potential new clients. Even if people don't show up you still have their number to call them.

Imagine the increase in income...

To see how you can build a $5000 a week semi-private business, check out this video → https://youtu.be/zIKrnzWLnu0

Bonus Chapter III
BUILD A SUCCESSFUL ONLINE FITNESS BUSINESS

With billions of people now online using social media, it seems every personal trainer and their dog wishes to do online personal training or sell products and services online. And why not? It gives you immediate access to potential clients and customers on a global scale, and it's leveraged, so you can be sitting in your bathers in a hammock sipping a cocktail in Fiji while you make money. If this is the case, why do ninety-eight percent of PTs fail to make a living online?

It's one thing to make some extra cash on the side selling a few meal plans or supplements online, it's another to make a living from it. This chapter is about how to make a living from a full time online business.

Now I could easily write an entire book just on this topic, (and perhaps some day I will), but since this is just one chapter, I will do my best to remove all the jargon and simply lay out the steps for how to build a 6-figure online fitness business in just months.

As you are already aware, I spent 12 years in the fitness industry building face-to-face businesses before I burned out. I was diagnosed with glandular fever and chronic fatigue. That's when I turned to online, and have been full-time online for over 6 years as I write this. Within just 8–9 months I built a 7-figure online fitness business and have built 3 x 7-figure online businesses since. In fact, our current online fitness business is literally weeks from hitting $2 million a year completely online; we are currently adding 6 figures every week to our income on auto-pilot, and it's forecast to be doing $5 million dollars a year by this Christmas.

Because we run online businesses, we were able to travel the world for two-and-a-half years straight living out of five star hotels, and created an amazing lifestyle. BUT its FU#@$%& HARD WORK!

Building an online business takes about four times longer than building a face-to-face one, and you need a lot more time and money to get it going. However, if you are prepared to put in the time, energy and money, you can make some great money and a good lifestyle.

In the following pages, I will share with you the simple steps to build a 6-figure online fitness business. Is it the best way? Maybe, maybe not! Is it the only way? Certainly not. I do believe it is the fastest way without borrowing money though, and we have used this system with countless clients to build an online income fast.

Maybe you want to launch online in your spare time or part time; that will work; you can still use these strategies. Perhaps you have been in the industry for a while or are looking for some freedom and you want to do online full time; this is definitely for you. Maybe you are an at-home parent or have kids and want to spend more time with the family, travel more, or have more leverage. In this chapter, I will lay out the road map to build to 6 figures online.

THE NUMBER 1 REASON MOST FAIL TO MAKE A LIVING ONLINE

I believe the main reason people fail to make a living online (enough income to cover your living expenses or more) is because they have this idea. They have an idea to launch a product like an eight-week challenge, or sell information, a detox, or meal plan. But the problem with all of those things is they don't create forecasted income. When you have a job and work as an employee, there is a false sense of security, because you know each week you will get a certain amount of money. Now, with the direct debit system you can do the same with your PT business. You can see, based on your current client base, how much your direct debt company will send you each week.

So, the key here is, if you want to make a living online, you need to forecast your income.

The main types of forecasted continuous income online are: sub-scriptions, memberships and coaching/consulting.

The challenge with subscriptions and memberships is you have to create a lot of content. videos, e-books etcetera. So, you have to put time and money into something and hope it sells.

However, if you were to sell coaching or consulting you could start making money immediately and good money. No, it's not passive income, but once you set up your value ladder, sales funnels and build a team, that too will come. My intention for this chapter is to show you how to make 6 figures online in the next 6 months anywhere in the world!

So, based on the coaching model, I have outlined 10 steps to create, launch and build a 6-figure online business in the next 6 months...

Here is a video that outlines exactly how you can build a 6-figure online fitness business in the next 6 months

➔ https://youtu.be/DrTzjxe67FU

Chapter Step 1) Create Your Coaching Package

All you really need to start selling your coaching online is a few things. When I launched my first coaching business online nearly eight years ago, I had pretty much no content. No videos, books, modules, tools or resources. Now we have thousands. All I knew is, I could help PTs build to six figures fast as I had done it many times.

To sell your online personal training service, you need to be able to show people exactly what they will get. I don't sell time, as in the sales part of this book, I always sell results. So, we charge $69–$399 a week for different programs.

To gain clarity on what exactly you will offer in your coaching program, simply begin deciding how much you want to charge each week. I suggest $49-$99 as a starting point. As you gain more clients and credibility you can charge more.

Once you have done that, you want to make checklist of exactly what your clients will receive for that price.

Simply see below for an example of one of our packages:

THE PROGRAM INCLUDES

- Monthly Personalized Meal Plans for EVERY MEAL, EVERY DAY - Suitable for vegetarians and Vegans. Includes recipes from our library as released
- Monthly Personalized Fitness Plans - weights, cardio & more for Each Day! NO Gym Membership required. Plus Video Exercise library as released
- The 7 Day Raw Detox Program with shopping lists, recipes, meal planners
- Accountability Sessions every 2 weeks over the phone or Skype to keep you on track, accountable and motivated. Plus we also design your plans.
- Your very own Coach & Fitness Expert committed to your personal results
- Become an athlete of the mind with our Mental Vitamins program to align values, stop self sabotaging habits, overcome doubts and fears, reframe limiting beliefs
- Exclusive access to the Facebook VIP Online Health retreat with fitness professionals and other participants of the program for 24/7 support
- Full Tracking with our networked app to monitor your nutrition & training
- Regular re-assessments including photos, weight & measurements
- Ongoing Facebook support, motivation and accountability
- Access to all our VIP Videos, events, webinars, recipes and more

www.quantumonlinepersonaltraining.com
www.facebook.com/quantumonlinepersonaltraining

Yes, I know I love PowerPoints—ha! I just think they look great.

You can see we use the same PowerPoint template for all packages and all services.

Take the time now to create your PowerPoint using the template provided.

IF you would like to gain FREE access to our complete Starter Kit for Online PTs with the actual templates and all these tools and more, simply visit here: freeonlineptstarterkit.com/

Chapter Step 2) Create Your Target Market Avatar

Once you have your visual aid you can show people what your service includes and for what price. Before you begin sales and marketing, it's super important to be clear about your target market. This is even more important online, because once you start paid advertising, the more clearly you can define your dream client, the more effectively you will be able to target them with your ads.

Start by creating an avatar. You know, like in a computer game where you choose your character, their clothes, hair colour, etcetera. Create an avatar as your dream client. Now of course not all your clients will be dream clients, especially in the beginning. In fact, I say you have to dig through the dirt to get to the gold. The more gold you find after digging the more you will attract.

So, name your avatar. Say it's Tom. Tom is a male millennial 24 years of age. He has a girlfriend but no kids. He is a tradesman and works sixty hour weeks on a salary of $75,000 a year. He has brown hair and lives in Sydney, Australia. Be very specific and clear.

Chapter Step 3) Create your Sign-up Process

Now you are clear on what program you are offering, you can show it to others; you know the cost and who you want as a client; all you need is really a means to collect their money and set up your online tools.

You can create online pre-exercise questionnaires, terms and conditions, websites etcetera. However, this section is focused on what you need to get started as quickly as possible to begin making money and growing your business. And all you really need to get started is a link to send your potential client so they can sign anywhere in the world, and you can receive weekly funds from them. The reason why I like weekly is because I like a consistent income; wouldn't you prefer a consistent income?

You have a few options. Many people use companies like PayPal and Stripe, which is fine, but at the end of the day they are pretty much online banks. The problem is you will be paid sporadically, and the tracking systems on them are good but not great. Also, more often than not, you have to wait longer to receive the funds in your actual bank account to access them. Don't get me wrong; we use them but for one-time international sales of products or courses.

For consistent income, I prefer to simply model what we do in our PT business; use a direct debit company. This way you can receive all the funds in one go every week, you have consistent income, you can forecast and budget more effectively, and you have more freedom to adjust payments and details. Not to mention the tracking systems are more in-depth and they have automatic debt recovery systems.

My suggestion is to create a free account with a direct debit company, or use the one you currently do for your PT business, and simply have them assist you in creating an online form. This way you simply send your potential client a link, and they can sign anywhere in the world on any touch screen device. Easy!

To be honest, the above three steps literally only take twenty-four to forty-eight hours, so you could be building an online client base and making money almost immediately. Then, as you build, you can create content, write blogs, books, create videos, do webinars etcetera.

Chapter Step 4) Set up Your Social Media

Over the past eight years I have built our Facebook groups and pages to over one million people collectively, including 100,000 Personal Trainers.

The process I'm going to share with you is modelled from more than a dozen eight-figure internet marketers who all use a similar philosophy. At this stage of your online business, you are not making much money, so your leverage will be time. By setting up your social media platform correctly, you can generate hundreds of quality leads every week for your business without spending a dime!

Everyday business owners of all kinds ask me what is better, a fan page or a group? Or how do I best set up my social media? The strategy I'm about to share with you in the following steps literally generates us 300-500 pre-qualified quality leads EVERY WEEK, as I write this book, and increasing all the time. We currently gain 15-20 high-ticket online coaching clients each week right now, adding an average of 6 figures to our income EVERY WEEK! Here is how we set our social media up to do this…

Here are the five key elements you want to use:

1. A community Facebook group
2. A VIP Facebook Group
3. A fan page
4. Your personal profile
5. A group chat

1. A Community Facebook Group

This group is a generic group to build a community of people and drive large numbers to the group. The number one intention is to use it to build an online community of pre-qualified potential clients and drive big numbers.

If you were to create a group named your business name—say I called it Jason Grossman's Personal Training, would that get more or less people naturally joining it and conversing than one called Fitness, Nutrition & Motivation?

Of course, the generic name will. This is a place that attracts people interested in the topic.

This group is an open group so it's easy to find. Yes, you will promote your business in there, and I will give you a plan for this shortly.

Its super important you lay out the rules:
1. No spamming, affiliate links or network marketing
2. No bullying, swearing or unsavory behavior
3. No outside links or bait.

I would actually create a Facebook group banner and have the rules on the banner. You can pay someone on www.fiverr.com six dollars to design it for you.

You can also set it up so when people request to join, they have to answer two to three questions that pre-qualify them, and you can choose to accept them or not.

The more explicitly you communicate the rules, the better this will work, and the more interaction created.

2. A Facebook VIP Group

This is a closed group that we personally use as a funnel to get clients online, a place for potential clients to see testimonials, content, and credible information, so they can do their due diligence. The primary intention is to use this as a funnel for new clients.

This is a closed group by invitation only. The only people we invite are potential clients, clients and ex-clients: anyone that downloads any of our e-books, kit, digital products, or is booked by one of our telemarketers for a free coaching consult.

Personally, I would call this the name of your business followed by VIPs. For example, ours is Quantum Body Transformation VIPs.

Again, you can pay six dollars to have a professional banner designed.

3. Facebook Fan Page

The primary intention of a fan page is so you can create Facebook ads. It's simple: the businesses online that make the most money are the ones that can spend the most on ads. You cannot create ads through any other platform, which is why you need a page. Creating virality and community on a page is getting harder all the time due to Facebook changing their algorithm a lot, and their edge-ranking system. So, we use our fan pages to generate leads and attract cold markets and our groups for warm markets. We add value, share social proof and content to transform them into hot market, then clients.

To create your fan page, have it open, and I would call it your business name. Have a professional banner made, and if you can, a profile pic of you with your ripped abs or bikini bod. A little superficial but that's what works!

4. Your Personal Profile

I'm guessing you will already have this, but how do you get the most out of it. What's the first word in your career title of Personal Trainer? Personal, right? Trying to keep business and personal separate online in the fitness industry is virtually impossible. You can use your personal profile to build your business. I have 5000 Facebook friends and 21,000 followers on my personal profile, so yes, you can. We will discuss how to use this in step 6.

5. Facebook VIP Chat

Unlike the Facebook group, this is an instant message chat. This chat is only for current paying clients. Once you have at least six to eight, add them in an instant chat so they can communicate and you can motivate and inspire them daily. You can set them up as running buddies, create games with prizes and keep them more accountable. Just be sure to get them to turn off their text notifications as it can run a little hot, but it's definitely worth it.

Overview

Once you have all of these set up, what we then do is record a welcome video and message so when people join the group, we can direct them to the video and message with the tools, free lead captures and rules. This is incredibly powerful in creating a community. If you check any of our groups and pages you will see they all have this. I want to make everyone feel a warm welcome, then offer them a free meal plan, e-book or resource to get them kick started.

Here is a bonus video on how to set up these groups

→ https://youtu.be/wRmixiC4cC4

Chapter Step 5) Generate 100 Leads with Your Official Launch

I remember about eight years ago sitting at my laptop in our first very humble office, and on my screen an advert from Kit-Kat (you know the chocolate bar) appeared. Kit-Kat were giving away a trip for two to Hawaii and it was free to enter. The trip was valued at $4997 USD.

So of course, I did what most would, I spent sixty seconds entering my details. A few weeks went by when I received an email from kit-Kat, saying unfortunately I didn't win the prize and congratulating the more than 500,000 people for entering the draw. That caught my attention; they added 500,000 people to their opt-in database, and they can now send promotions and information too whenever they like, all for just $5000. Well, plus the advertising costs. Do you know how much you would have to pay on social media or google to get that number? It's a lot more than a few thousand.

This got me thinking. We did a prize draw for PT to win a trip for two to Bali from Perth Western Australia. It cost us less than $2000 and we generated 800 opt-in leads. We added more than 40 sessions a week and 6 figures ($2000 a week) to our income from that one promotion!

Ever since then I have been a massive fan of prize draws. And use it to launch any new venture or business.

Imagine if you offered every Facebook friend, every group and page member, everyone you have a phone number for and everyone you have an email address for the opportunity to win eight weeks free coaching with you to celebrate your launch. Below I have provided a step-by-step process which, if you use it, will give you 100+ leads in your first week in your online coaching business. THEN after you draw a winner, you simply offer the remaining 99 people a free consult to have the opportunity to upsell them. This will give you five to ten clients in your first few weeks when done correctly, because you know if people entered the draw they must be interested in the service in some way shape or form!

Here are the steps for your success...

Step 1) Create a free account at http://eventbrite.com

Step 2) Create event with description on Eventbrite using the example below. Once you set up the event you will need to go to 'manage event', then click on the order form on the left and be sure to tick the two boxes so that way you are getting everyone's phone number, or you cannot ring and confirm!

If you are looking for a quick way to create an image as in the example below, I use the free app called Adobe Spark. The below image took me literally sixty seconds to create.

Here is a script if you wish to copy and paste:
How would you like to lose weight, tone up, increase your energy, or put on lean muscle mass?

We are very excited to announce we are giving one lucky person the opportunity to WIN 8 weeks free coaching with one of our experts, which includes, fitness plans, meal plans, mind-set and more.

To be in the running, we only have 50 spots, so be quick and enter your name number and email for the chance to win.

Yours in Health and Fitness, *Jason Grossman.*

Step 3) Create Facebook event with link to Eventbrite for online registration through your personal profile, and one for each of your groups. If you have more than 500 friends you may need to create more than one event.

Simply copy and paste the details from your Eventbrite event and paste them into your Facebook event, AND add the link to your Eventbrite registration page.

You will notice at the bottom of the example below is a Bitly URL web link. I have shortened the Eventbrite link as it looks ugly. To shorten your Eventbrite link simply visit www.bitly.com

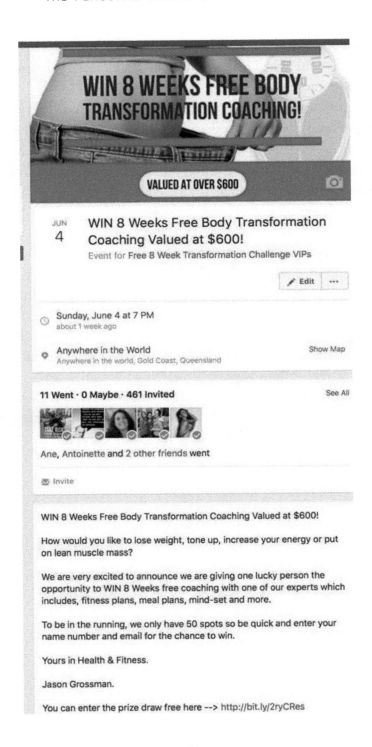

WIN 8 WEEKS FREE BODY TRANSFORMATION COACHING!

VALUED AT OVER $600

JUN
4

WIN 8 Weeks Free Body Transformation Coaching Valued at $600!

Event for Free 8 Week Transformation Challenge VIPs

Edit   ...

Sunday, June 4 at 7 PM
about 1 week ago

Anywhere in the World   Show Map
Anywhere in the world, Gold Coast, Queensland

11 Went · 0 Maybe · 461 Invited   See All

Ane, Antoinette and 2 other friends went

Invite

WIN 8 Weeks Free Body Transformation Coaching Valued at $600!

How would you like to lose weight, tone up, increase your energy or put on lean muscle mass?

We are very excited to announce we are giving one lucky person the opportunity to WIN 8 Weeks free coaching with one of our experts which includes, fitness plans, meal plans, mind-set and more.

To be in the running, we only have 50 spots so be quick and enter your name number and email for the chance to win.

Yours in Health & Fitness.

Jason Grossman.

You can enter the prize draw free here --> http://bit.ly/2ryCRes

Step 4) Post on your personal wall a link to your Facebook event, and tag all your clients so their friends see it through their newsfeed. Also post in every group and page you have.

You will post twice a day in each Facebook event. A social proof and an add value post. Client testimonials, results, videos, images. Also articles, blogs, videos, info graphics, etcetera.

Step 5) Create a free www.mailchimp.com email marketing account and create a list for your entire database, and copy EVERY email address you have in there; then send a bulk email with a link to your Eventbrite event.

Simply visit the above website link and click 'sign-up free' as in the document below the ad.

Step 6) download ExcelSMS (otherwise known as SA Group Text) from iPhone or android and send a bulk text to everyone you have a phone number for with a link to Eventbrite each week.

Once you download this app, simply create your text database by following the instructions in the video tutorial below, which my partner Kailey recorded with clear instructions.

See the tutorial here: https://www.youtube.com/watch?v=OZIM-LB6Q7jc&feature=youtu.be

Step 7) Have all your attendees on the Facebook event invite all their friends (send them a group Facebook message asking them and also who they will be bringing). You can offer an incentive, free PT session or something else, or even a prize draw.

Step 8) Get yourself a clipboard and piece of paper made up on an Excel spreadsheet and printed. Include name and number at the top. Place it on the clipboard. Then you are going to register ALL of your PT Clients plus one friend each on that clipboard, then go home and enter their details on the Eventbrite. This gives you control so you are not just relying on them visiting the rego page. ALSO, be sure to register anyone else you come into face-to-face contact with. If you have PTs working for you, give them a clipboard each.

Step 9) After the prize draw, announce the winner; I use the google random number selector. Then call everyone who didn't win and use the prize draw script in the prospect and booking system to book them in for a free consult and sell them PT.

Remember, once you have done the prize draw, to ring everyone who didn't win and book them in for a free consult, and use the sales script in the next step.

Chapter Step 6) Create Your Sales System
Once you are ready to begin selling your coaching service, wouldn't you agree that having a tested script to use would drastically increase your conversion rates? How much would it suck if you took the time to set everything up, begin marketing and booking appointments to simply get no after no. Especially when you know sure, you want to make money, it's a real business but you are also doing it to help others and impact lives.

Over the past eight years of doing and selling online coaching, we have sold and delivered online personal training, online body trans-formation coaching, business coaching for fitness business owners, life coaching, coaching for online coaches, mind set coaching, NLP coaching, and wealth creation coaching.

The team and I have tested dozens of scripts over 5000 showed consults to determine what works best. I have refined and perfected a script over the past eight years to sell online personal training, and when followed it will give you an eighty percent conversion rate—imagine!

I contemplated not adding these into this book, but this is a library and there's so much to cover in the online chapter I cannot include everything. But I know these sales scripts could be the most valuable thing in this chapter that will have the most profound impact on your growth.

On the upcoming pages are the actual scripts our coaches use in our business. I have given them to you openly because I truly want to see you win, and I believe with cooperation rather than competition we can put a dent in the obesity epidemic!

You can also find these scripts in the free starter kit for Online PTs. I suggest you print them and read them word for word. That's the beauty of selling online coaching as opposed to face-to-face selling of PT.

Face to face, you have to try and memorize everything. Whereas doing it online, you can simply read it, as you will be on a call so they can't see you—easy. And even if you did choose video (we found it better not to as people open up more) you could still read them.

I understand that when reading a script, at first it doesn't feel natural, because the truth is, you would write something different. But why guess and try to work it out for yourself when we have had hundreds of people test these, so we know they are duplicable, and if you choose to use them you can win big! Trust in the process, they have been tested thousands of times.

We do an initial free thirty-minute consult, then a free thirty-minute follow-up and close in the follow-up. Traditionally, we always sell in the first contact in sales, but after testing this thousands of times, we have found selling in the follow-up has more than a double percentage conversion rate!

Here are the scripts:

FREE TRANSFORMATION CONSULT

Step 1) Build Massive Rapport (5 minutes maximum)
Ask open-ended questions to connect with them personally (not results related)

Family/occupation/where they live etcetera.... find commonality and connect!

Do you mind if I share a bit about myself?

Share briefly:
- Your personal journey
- Your career and experience journey
- Your qualifications

Step 2) Their Nutrition, Fitness and Psychology

So <NAME> do you exercise at the moment?
How often?
What do you do when you exercise?
DO you go to the gym?
Whats your favourite way to train/exercise?
'What do you like the least?
And what about your eating, how is your eating?
What did you have for breakfast, lunch and dinner today?
Do you think you eat healthy?
IF you want to change your body, would you say you need to change your eating and training?
Are you prepared to do that?

PSYCHOLOGY!!

One of the things that makes us different is our focus on your mind-set, reframing limiting beliefs, realigning incongruent values, overcoming fears and doubts, and eliminating any self-sabotage or toxic habits and behaviours. So, what would you say your mental strengths are?
And what about your mental weaknesses?
WE CAN DEFINITELY ASSIST WITH THAT.

Step 3) Their Desired Results

WHAT

So <NAME> Tell me about the results you want to achieve. WHAT exactly would you like to do?

How much weight exactly?

WHERE

Clothing size?

Where exactly would you like to achieve it?

Select a number 1 priority

WHEN

When exactly would you like to achieve it by?

WHY

Why would you like to achieve it by then?

HOW

How would you feel if you didn't achieve it by then?

BUT how would you feel if you did achieve it by then?

Can I ask a question?

'Why exactly is it SO Important for you to achieve it by then?'

'Great; what would it truly mean for you as a person to achieve it?'

'On a Scale of 1 to 10, 10 being the most important, how important is it to you?'

'And that will truly mean for you?'

'<NAME> If you keep doing what you have been doing up until now, do you think you will achieve it by then?'

'NO; right, so we need to make some changes; are you prepared to make those changes?'

Step 4) Give them the clarity and unloading exercise to complete

We are very particular about who we choose to work with, so we like to connect with someone a few times before we decide. I'm going to invite you to complete what we call a clarity and unloading exercise in the next forty-eight hours before our next chat, then go from there.

Right now, you have a lot of stuff going through your mind, like what do you want to do, how to do it, when you want to do it by. SO, this afternoon I'm going to send you a quick video tutorial explaining how to do the exercise, to give you more clarity and direction.

Basically, you are just going to make a list of all the outcomes you wish to achieve in the next six months for your health, lifestyle and physical goals. Then place all those items into the columns in the spreadsheet which I will also send to you via Facebook, giving you a basic action plan for next six months.

If you can send that back to me before our next chat on Facebook, then we can determine the next steps, the "how to", and if we are going to be a good fit working together.

How do you feel about completing that exercise?

Why do you think it will be a great idea for you to complete this?

(CONFIRM AND STACK)

Step 5) book them in for 48-72 hours later (at the latest)
Always confirm every appointment the evening before via a Facebook message and/or text.

IMPORTANT: Before you hang up, be sure to add them as a Facebook friend, AND also add them to your VIP group, and be sure to welcome them with a tag (no need for pic).

SEND THEM THIS:

Hey (NAME) was great to connect ☺

Please find below the simple goal spreadsheet to complete and the quick vid tutorial with specific instructions.

If you can please send this back to me on Facebook before our appointment, that will be great.

(include YouTube link to video tutorial)

FREE BODY TRANSFORMATION FOLLOW-UP PROCESS

Step 1) re-establish rapport (spend 5 minutes connecting personally)

Ask what they did on the weekend.

How have their last few days been?

Step 2) Determine their 3 biggest health/lifestyle goals

So how did you go with sitting down thinking about the outcomes you want to achieve?

How did you find the process?

What I want to do today is establish what are your TOP three health and lifestyle outcomes you wish to achieve in the next six months, and even greater than that, If I was to help you achieve just one thing and one thing only, what would your absolute biggest goal for the next six months be?

Make sure it's specific and can be measured.

Step 3) Create pleasure and pain, giving them awareness of the fact that they need guidance and change

I know I asked you these questions last time, but I'd like to ask them again, now that you have a bit more clarity and direction.

So, why is it so important you achieve (NAME THEIR TOP GOAL) in the next six months?

What would it really mean for you to achieve that?

How would you feel if in six months you are still exactly where you are right now?

BUT how would you feel if you had the right support and guidance and you did achieve what you want in next six to twelve months?

If you keep doing exactly what you have been doing up until now, do you think you are guaranteed to be where you want to be?

So, you've got to make some changes right? Are you prepared to make those changes?

How do you think having a coach or a mentor to guide you with meal plans, fitness plans, accountability and mind set will help make this easier and more of a reality for you?

Step 4) Clarify the program and how it works
So, If we choose to work with you, this is how the coaching program works:

Each week for the next four weeks, we will have a coaching session. Then it's AT LEAST fortnightly after that. Next week when we start, we will organize a time to create your first monthly meal plan, which will include every meal for the week. The following week we create a personalized fitness program; then the week after we take you through the mental vitamins program to align your psychology for success and become an athlete of the mind.

You then continue to receive a monthly personalized meal plan and monthly personalized fitness plan. We use a fitness tracking app to monitor your results to ensure that even when you reach plateaus we can determine the strategy or mind-set necessary to break through it.

Then even though this program is a minimum of three months, we keep working together until you succeed. Everyone we choose to work with either gets incredible results or they quit!

So how does that process and that journey sound to you?

What do you like most about this process?

Awesome. Well, if we choose to work with you, everything in this program is just $69 a week for everything, including all the personalized plans, tracking. and regular coaching sessions…

Step 5) The Close

As mentioned, we are very particular about who we choose to work with, so there's just a few questions I have before I decide.

First question: if I choose to work with you, will you be coachable, show up to the sessions, stick to the process, not blame, make excuses or complain, and just get it done?

Secondly, I want to work with people that are hungry and made a decision to win, so If I choose to work with you, would you say you have the desire to do whatever it takes to make this work?

The third thing is probably the most important. I want to work with people that have mental toughness. You know life will knock you down and obstacles will get in the way. In fact, over the upcoming weeks you will contemplate quitting coaching, and perhaps even make the decision to quit. But if I choose to work with you I want to know you have the mental toughness to keep getting back up when knocked down, push through the sticking points, and never ever quit on your goals and dreams. Would you say you have that mental toughness?

That's great. Now lastly, if I was to give you one last chance to convince me why I should choose to work with you, what would you say to me?

BIG PAUSE!!!

Ok I believe in you, and I know we can do big things together, so I'm happy to move forward and get you started. Do you have any more questions or are you just ready to get started?

Step 6) Make an appointment and complete their direct debit form

Great, let's book you in for next week then I will explain next steps.

BOOK THEM IN FOR NEXT WEEK.

NOW OPEN THE DIRECT DEBIT FORM IN THIS LINK: (Insert your Direct Debit link)

OK great, all I need to secure your spot is a few details; what is your email address? (ENTER IT INTO THE DD FORM). Also enter their number, which you know.

And what is your address? (Enter that in).

Lastly do you have a debit card or credit card?

Then enter their details and submit the form.

When it goes through:

Congratulations and welcome aboard. What are you most excited about?

Awesome. Well, I look forward to talking to you in our next session to create your meal plan. In the meantime, if you have any questions, I'm always here for you.

NOW welcome them with a message, tag them and a photo to your open group, VIP group and fan page on Facebook.

Chapter Step 7) Execute the Facebook Marketing Plan

Once your social media is set up, the next questions seem to be: what do I post, when do I post, how often do I post?

Social media allows us to use the most powerful form of marketing on the globe—word of mouth. The problem is people don't know how to use this effectively through the process known as network marketing. I'm not talking about multi-level marketing companies; I'm talking about the strategy of network marketing. The ability to build networks through your current network.

Let's say you are connected to 1000 people on social media and they too are connected to 1000 people, the real question is not, how do I get in front of my network of 1000 people; the real question is, how do you get in front of your networks to a network of one million people?

1000 x 1000 = 1,000,000 (one million people)

Isn't that crazy! And to make it even crazier, we can do this without spending a single dollar.

Here is how:

I have created a Facebook plan template that you can simply use as a guide to take the guesswork out. What to post and when to post...

You can get the Free Planner here → ptsocialmediaplan.com/

You can also watch this video on how to use the planner

→ https://youtu.be/PKC-y7jkAB0

In this Facebook planner, I have offered a simple but easy to follow 7-day plan with what to post on your groups, page and profile, and when.

It's important to understand the five steps which are covered on the above video and also the content.

There are really five main types of posts.

1. Social proof
2. Add value content
3. Social recognition
4. Entertainment
5. Marketing

Social proof

- Written testimonials
- Before and after pics
- Video testimonials
- Group bootcamp pics
- In-action vids and pics with you and clients.

Add value content

- Blogs/articles
- Webinars
- Videos
- Recipes
- Workout routines
- E-books
- Free planners (meal plans/fitness plans).

Social recognition
- Happy birthday
- Welcome new clients
- Recognition for achievement, activity or commitment
- Client of the week/month
- Winner of competition/prize draw
- Welcome to the group
- Team member of the week month
- Team member recognition.

Entertainment
- Memes
- Funny videos
- Live videos.

Marketing
- Events
- 2 free consults
- Challenges.

This is all covered in more depth in the video. I would strongly suggest grabbing the free marketing planner and watching the video to implement this effectively; it is incredibly powerful. Really, I believe social media should be all about people. We want to make our social media eighty percent about our clients and team by recognizing them every chance we can, elevating them, connecting them, and creating a community. If you follow this Facebook planner 100% you will generate thirty to fifty leads every week without spending a dollar!

Facebook Planner

	Monday	Tuesday	Wednesday	Thursday	Friday	Saturday	Sunday
6-9am							
Personal Profile	Live Video/share	Motivational Video	In action video	Client Shout Out/Test	Live Video/share		
FanPage	Branded Graphic	Routine	Recipe	Branded Graphic	Question		
Open Group	Client Shout Out/Test	Poll	Branded Graphic	Client Shout Out/Test		GYM POST	
VIP Group	Opinion/Question	Opinion/Question	Client Shout Out/Test	In action photos			
12-1pm							
Personal Profile	Client Shout Out/Test	2 Free Consults/First 3	Live Video/share	In action video	Question		
FanPage	Client Shout Out/Test	Branded Graphic	In action photos	Client Shout Out/Test	Branded Graphic		
Open Group	Branded Graphic	Client Shout Out/Test	Client Shout Out/Test	Branded Graphic	Client Shout Out/Test		
VIP Group	Recipe	Client Shout Out/Test	In action pics	Routine	BLOOPER Vid/Pic		
730-930pm							
Personal Profile	Facebook Event	Live Video/share	BLOG	Live Video/share	RELAX/OR		
FanPage	Client of Week	New Ad: OPT In	Branded Graphic	In action photos	What u doin this W/E	RELAX/OR	Branded Graphic
	Facebook Event	Facebook Event	Facebook Event	Facebook Event	Facebook Event		
Open Group	Client of Week	Branded Graphic	Opinion/Question	Recipe	Branded Graphic		
	welcomes	welcomes	welcomes	welcomes			
VIP Group	Facebook Event	welcomes	2 Free consults/first 3	Routine	Branded Graphic	Question for week	welcomes
	Client of Week	In action video	Client Shout Out/Test	Facebook Event	RELAX/OR	Motivational Vid	
	welcomes	welcomes	welcomes	Poll	What u doin this W/E		
	Facebook Event			Facebook Event			

Daily

personal profile	Facebook	Open Grup	VIP Group	FB Event
3-5 x day	7-10 x day	3-5 x day	5-7 x day	Post 2-3 x day

Social Proof

testimonials	daily
shout outs	daily
welcome/birthdays	daily
client of week	1 x week
in action pics	Blog

Quality Content

Graphic	1 x day
Other Video	1 x day
recipe	1-2 week
routine	1-2 x week
Blog	weekly/fortnightly

Add Value Marketing

sales funnel/opt in	2-3 x week
first 3 strategy	2 x week
events	1 month
Webinar/team call	1 month
try before you buy offer	1 x week
FB advertising	daily

Interaction

Poll/question	1-2 x week
opinion	1-2 x week

EVENTS:

- Social
- Charity
- Info Night
- Work Shop
- Webinar
- Prize Draw

Chapter Step 8) Create your Sales Funnels to Generate Hundreds of Leads a Week

If you want to build a large online business of any kind, you need to build a list. A distribution list of controlled traffic. Email list, phone list, social media, YouTube and Facebook bot (covered in next step)

The main difference between advertising and marketing is that with marketing, you capture someone's details in order to flip the power dynamics, and you have the control and ability to contact them.

Without some sort of lead capture form, this will be very difficult. The social media and network marketing strategies previously covered are a great way to generate quality leads, but if you want to build a large online business, you want to build a massive list. At present, we generate about 1000 leads a week online for our coaching business. We have a plan to be generating 2000+ leads a week within the next three to six months. Although a few hundred come through social media directly, seventy to eighty percent of our list is built through sales funnels.

Although traditional websites are still quite popular, to be honest they are completely unnecessary for lead generation or an online business. But don't take my word for it check out any internet marketer that make at least eight figures ($10,000,000 Million) a year. Ninety-nine percent of top internet marketers will say something similar.

We are conditioned to believe we need a website, and yes, they can have their uses, but in today's fast paced web, they are not necessary. We don't currently use a traditional website for any of our four online businesses, and we have a list of around one million people including 100,000 Personal Trainers.

We even used to run a business making hundreds of thousands of dollars a year selling logos and websites to PTs. It just didn't feel ethical anymore to sell PTs websites when there is a better way.

The better way is using sales funnels. A single page web page that you can drive traffic to generate leads and make sales. Once people enter in their details for your free offer, not only are they added to your email and phone list, but you can add back-end digital products or other services to monetize it and spend more money on advertising. We currently have nearly fifty of these generating 1000-1500 pre-qualified leads a week and growing all the time.

I understand many people are adamant about having a traditional website, and if you want one and think it looks good, go for it, that's great. I would also suggest doing some research into the world's top internet marketers and model what they do. As I write this paragraph, our online coaching business is literally weeks away from hitting $2,000,000 a year in sales without a traditional website, and will be yielding $5,000,000 consistent income by Christmas!

I have spent 100 hours designing four sales funnel templates you can use personally to generate hundreds of leads online without spending hundreds of hours designing a website or thousands of dollars paying someone to create one.

1. Free meal plan funnel
2. Free e-book funnel
3. 2 free online consults funnel
4. Free prize draw funnel

To get FREE access to all four of these funnels to use as you wish, simply download the FREE Starter Kit for Online Personal Trainers here → freeonlineptstarterkit.com/

Also, here is a bonus video on how to set these four funnels up → https://youtu.be/vqv3vZpekw4

Included in the Free Starter kit is also a free trial to the software we use. Everything you need to set this up ready to go is in the free starter kit.

Chapter Step 9) Begin Facebook Advertising
OK, so you now have your sales funnels set up, and you can generate leads online, but how do you drive traffic to them? The best bang for

buck with advertising I know of right now is Facebook advertising. Honestly, if this is something you struggle to wrap your head around, I would pay someone to help out. We have just connected with an amazing agency in the US that make more than $10,000,000 a year in sales from Facebook ads. Even though we do well with Facebook advertising, I want the best experts assisting me. I also paid a coach to assist me in creating our book funnels, spending tens of thousands of dollars.

However, to get you started, I want to show you how to create your basic Facebook ad campaigns for your four sales funnels on the previous step. This is why I recorded this one-hour video for you to watch on how to create your Facebook ad campaigns specific to the four previous funnels. If you follow it you will generate 100-200 leads every week, hands down!

You can watch the Facebook Advertising Video here → https://youtu.be/H5Ob5n3-lBI

Chapter Step 10) Create a Facebook Bot & Online Virtual Coach
As I write this chapter right now, the hottest thing online is perhaps a Facebook messenger bot. But what is a Bot?

Imagine you are marketing to generate leads and you are asking for people's contact phone number or email address. They have to enter those details into some kind of lead capture or form and then once they do, you can now text, ring or email them until they choose to opt out.

To build a service business I believe phone calls are super important, but texting people more than perhaps once a month may become spammy.

The problem with email is that these days, due to social media, less and less people are using email. Ask 10 millennials in a room who uses email, and I would be surprised if any hands are raised. So only a small number of people you email will actually see your email. Only about eight percent of people we email see or read that email.

What if you could build a list of people you could send a private message to on Facebook at any time, and Facebook would allow it?

That's what a bot will allow you to do. We currently have about 7000 people opted into our Facebook bots, which means right now I can send a Facebook private message to more than 7000 people at one time. Imagine the extra leads, consults, sales, new clients. And a whopping eighty-two to eighty-eight percent of people you send the message to see the message. This is huge.

The other cool thing is to have people opt in; you don't need to retrieve any information. All they need to do is comment on a post on your fan page—are you kidding me.

Most Facebook advertising we do currently is to promote bots, because Facebook are limiting the amount of views posts get with links or lead capture links in the post, and as I write this Facebook promote the interactive posts that seem natural. We have 100-300 people every day opt into our bots. You can send welcome videos, set up autoresponders, and even do what we have done, which is set it up as an online virtual coach. Imagine creating an automatic system via your Facebook fan page where people can automatically interact with your content, communicate, generate leads, have appointments made, make sales, and all on auto-pilot. That's the power of a Facebook bot.

If you opt into any of our bots we have put literally hundreds of hours of content in there. Plus, we can funnel people into our funnels, email list, phone list, Facebook VIP group and YouTube channel!

If you don't have a bot I think you are crazy, and who knows how long Facebook will even allow this. As you read this, it may already have been stopped, hopefully they are still going.

Here is a video in-depth on how to set up a Facebook messenger Bot for your fitness business → https://youtu.be/HyGm-x1NTAo

LAUNCH YOUR ONLINE FITNESS BUSINESS

If you are serious about building an online fitness business in your spare time, part time or even full time, I truly believe the fastest way to build a forecasted income that can create a living for you is via these steps. You don't need massive websites and content and to look flashy, you have everything you need to coach people in your mind. I guarantee if you follow these steps it's possible for you to make a 6- even 7-figure online business.

If you seek any further assistance feel free to chat with one of our expert coaches to see how we can build you to 6- even 7-figures online here → https://freebusinesshealthcheck.com/

ALSO, here is the video on how to build a 6-Figure Online Fitness Business in the next 6 months → https://youtu.be/DrTzjxe67FU

BONUS STEP 11) Scaling your Online Fitness Business - Building a Team and Outsourcing
If you are happy simply building a client base for yourself, the previous steps when done correctly will take you to six figures plus.

However, if you want to build a larger online fitness business, perhaps even seven figures or more, not only will you need a full value ladder of products and services, but also a team. So, in part I will share how you can begin to do that.

Building an online client base is cool, as you have a leveraged income from anywhere in the world, but the truth is you still need to work and it's not passive income. So how do you scale and automate your online business?

To be honest, sales funnels, Facebook bot and online adverts are all a form of scaling, but if you want a serious income you really want to build a team. Here is the model we use that will take us to an 8-figure online business.

Step 1 – Get yourself 12-14 clients. Doing 14 consults a week. 2-3 new clients a week.

Step 2 – At this stage you want to begin to remove yourself from more menial tasks. But you want to pay someone else as little as possible for IPA (income producing activities) at this stage. I highly recommend getting a good English speaking, bubbly telemarketer. There are hundreds of companies in the Philippines, and you can easily pay someone $6-8 an hour for 20 hours of calls to start. This will give you 20+ consults a week.

Step 3 – Hire your first coach – This person will also do 14 consults, giving you 28 consults a week and will double the speed of growth of your business. Train them to sell and treat them like a business partner rather than an employee. Put them on a pedestal and make your business about them. I even drop the hint that if they play their cards right they could be head coach down the track.

In fact, that's the goal to build a big, powerful sales force. We currently have 10 coaches doing 100 consults a week that will double in the next 6 months. Imagine 200 consults every week in your business on autopilot. We average 15-20 new clients every week, that's an increase of 6 figures every week, and the speed at which it's building is gaining momentum.

I add a $99 kick-start fee to the package, so every sale they make they get that commission. I want my coaches to earn 6 figures plus. I don't just help them with their clients and business but also their dreams, whatever they may be.

Step 4 – Hire your second coach and get them selling. Also increase your telemarketer to full time (40 hours a week) as 3 x 14 = 42. Between the 3 of you that's 42 consults a week. As you are making more income you can put more money into Facebook and YouTube adverts to generate enough leads to provide the telemarketer. 100 a week part time and 200 a week full time.

We are currently about to hire our 3rd and 4th telemarketer and 10th, 11th and 12th coach. We have 100+ consults every week booked and add 15-20 clients a week, adding 6 figures a week, as above, on autopilot. Within 3-6 months we will be booking 200 consults a week and adding $250,000 a week to our income on autopilot. And this doesn't include any of our other income streams or businesses; imagine...

Step 5 – Hire a 3rd coach and appoint them as head coach. You will work with them, and they will work with other coaches. At this point if you have 3 coaches who can sell doing 50-60 consults a week you can cut back on selling. And begin to focus on larger action items, live events, publishing books, investing, expansion, building a large team, or even travelling and spending time with family.

Step 6 – at this stage you may need a few other team members. I would outsource them all.

Here are some you may need:

a. A customer service manager to take care of all clients and their accounts, phone calls or payment changes

b. A bookkeeper if you don't have one

c. Optionally a finance manager to take care of all accounts payable

d. A virtual assistant to take care of your admin, data entry, lists, schedule

e. We have a sales funnel assistant to do all the sales funnels, email autoresponders, emails, and changes to funnels include the tech stuff I have no clue about

f. A social media manager who does your posting, Facebook ads etc. You could also pay a VA in the beginning to do the basics.

g. If you want to do this is a big way you can hire someone to do your job and completely remove yourself from the company like I am doing; pay them six figures and make millions a year on autopilot. Use the excess money to build a property portfolio, investment business portfolio and share portfolio, as we are. Also, we love to travel so we do this a lot.

Is this the only way to build a large scaled online business? Definitely not! Is it the fastest? I don't know; maybe, maybe not. But does this work? You bet your ass it does, and in a BIG way. Once you have a sales team of 3-10+ coaches selling every week it absolutely EXPLODES!! Official term!

OVERVIEW

Again, I feel I have left out a lot of information in this chapter. I really wanted to give you as much bang for your buck and focus on the simple yet powerful action items which, if you apply them, can assist you on your journey to building a 6-, 7- even multiple 7-figure online fitness business. It's possible. It's what we do. We actually have a coaching program called the 7-figure program where we show business owners how to build a 7-figure online business fast!

Any questions, feel free to reach out to one of our amazing expert coaches for two free coaching sessions to see how we can build your dream online business...

Bonus Chapter IV
BUILD A SUCCESSFUL PT STUDIO

Many personal trainers have the dream of one day owning their own studio or gym. As you read this, you may already have a studio. If you want to have your own studio or gym, this simple yet pragmatic chapter may assist you on your journey. If you are reading this and don't desire to have your own gym or studio, I would highly recommend doing it, even if it's as a business owner or investor, to gain the experience of running a real business.

I have had the opportunity to be a part of opening literally hundreds of studios and gyms, and to be honest I love it. I buy gyms and studios as an investor to build a portfolio of business investments on autopilot also.

To break this down into digestible pieces, I'm going to cover this chapter in three phases.

1. Getting market ready: preparing to purchase or invest in your own studio or gym
2. Launching and opening your studio: how to open it profitably
3. Scaling and automating your studio: creating freedom and duplication.

Again, I could literally write an entire book just on this topic, and again, who knows, one day I may. Since this is just one chapter, I cannot cover everything it takes to launch and build a scaled studio comprehensively, but I can definitely equip you with the main points you need to open, launch and scale your studio as I have done hundreds of times.

I believe the main reason many PTs don't open their own studio or gym is because they simply don't know how, through lack of belief, doubt, or because it seems like a daunting task. To be honest, opening your own studio is not that big a task once you know what you are doing. I understand it's not for everyone, but if you are entrepreneurial and like the idea of your own location, I highly recommend it. As a business owner, I want a multitude of products and services in my business. We have gyms, Pilates studios, online coaching, and dozens of products and services in several different industries.

Just because I don't enjoy delivering it or don't like something, it doesn't mean I dismiss it. I'm not a huge fan of Zumba personally, but many people are. When it was really hot and in demand, we implemented it into our business model, and hundreds would attend every week, creating a 6-figure income for the business on autopilot.

But everything we do is to scale so it can work without us. And if you begin with that end in mind, you will be surprised how big a business you can actually build. Heck, you could even launch your own franchise. If your dreams don't scare you they are not big enough!

OWNING A STUDIO WITH MEMBERS AND BUILDING A PORTFOLIO OF GYMS

One of the great things about owning your own studio or gym is capital growth, equity—it's something you can resell. If you build a team of trainers in a big box gym, the majority of the time you cannot sell it for what it's truly worth. And try going to the bank and saying your business is worth a certain amount!

Whereas when you have a finite gym or studio you can increase its capital growth, and use it as equity to borrow money to invest in property or other things. It adds to your net worth and you can begin to create true wealth.

For example, we buy franchises already established that are barely profitable. Then we refine the systems, marketing and team, and increase the business of the gym ten to twenty times.

This is why I suggest buying a 24/7 studio or gym as a starting point. With around 500 members. It is already established and has the foundation.

I recently came across a gym that had 500 members and a small team, with no real PT culture. It was doing about $360,000 a year turnover, but its net profit for last year was only $11,000. Across the board it's pretty similar but will change slightly country to country. In the fitness industry the value of a gym or studio is roughly 3.8–4.2 times the annual profit. For example, this gym was doing $11,000 profit, so it was selling for $45,000. (Always be sure to get a professional when valuing)

This means I can purchase this gym at a mere $45,000—that's it. I can implement marketing systems to double the memberships in 12 months to 1000 members. I can build a team of 5 PTs doing 200 sessions a week and take this business to $1,000,000 turnover in 12–18 months. How do I know this? I've done it so many times. That business would be doing around $180,000-$240,000 profit which means I could sell this business for $720,000–$960,000. WOW!

That's a 15-20 times increase in just 12 months. Plus, I could go to the bank, have it valued, and use this as equity to invest in property or my next investment business. Because these are investment gyms and we build a portfolio, I don't need the money, so 100% of the profits go can go into charity and reinvesting. You can be a millionaire in under three years using this strategy just buying one gym a year. We are investing in 3–5 every year as one of our portfolios, additional to our property portfolio, shares (stocks if in US) portfolio, and other business investments. This is also on top of the online coaching business doing millions a year in sales.

I'm not using these big numbers to impress you or intimidate you, quite the opposite. My goal is to show you how to build to 6 figures, 7 figures, then become a millionaire within 3 years. In fact, that's what our business coaching program for fitness business owners is designed to do.

1. 6 figures in 90 days
2. $250,000K in 6 months
3. 7 figures in 18 months
4. Millionaire within 3 years.

If you are hungry and ambitious and want to build a large fitness business, feel free to reach out to one of our coaches to begin this journey.

If you would like to take this path there are five things you really want to know before making the commitment.

Before I share them with you I would highly recommend that before making any decision, you get yourself a team of experts:
- Business coach specific to the fitness industry
- Solicitor with experience in gyms/studios
- Accountant
- Business broker – with experience in the industry.

The 5 things you want to know before committing to a buying a gym
1. Franchise agreement and terms
2. Lease agreement and terms
3. Equipment agreement and terms
4. Profit and loss statements
5. Team dynamics and culture.

FRANCHISE AGREEMENT AND TERMS

When investing in or buying an established franchise there will be a current agreement. It may be 3, 5, 7 years or some other length of time. It's important before investing in a gym you know when the franchise fee is next due, and when the term is over. Because there is a massive difference between an initial fee cost and a renewal cost.

For example, a franchise I recently looked at charges $80,000 for the 7-year franchise fee. The franchise I was looking at was due to renew the franchise agreement in just 5 months.

If I had purchased this gym now, I would have forked out a whopping $80,000 for a fee in just a few months' time.

Instead I negotiated with the gym owner for them to renew the franchise agreement then add that cost to the buying price.

This makes no difference to the seller because I'm covering the cost. But instead of paying $80,000 in 6 months for a new 7-year franchise agreement. It was just $7000. That's a lot of money. The owner simply renewed the franchise agreement and added that to the total buying cost. Make sense? So be sure to find out when the franchise agreement is up, what are the terms, and of course have your solicitor look over it.

LEASE AGREEMENT AND TERMS

Obviously, when buying a studio or gym franchise, the property is a separate business, generally with a separate owner. Even if it's not it will usually be a different entity (trust or company).

What this means is you will generally pay rent to whoever owns the building or their property manager.

When handover takes place and you take ownership of the gym or studio franchise, sometimes you will need to sign a new lease agreement, sometimes you will take over the existing.

It could be 1, 2, or even 5 years, with an additional option to extend the lease. I want the shortest lease possible because I buy gyms low and sell them high or even lock in lines of credit high to borrow against the equity to reinvest.

Personally, I don't sign anything longer than 2 years, 3 years maximum if there is potential for massive growth.

What's really important here is one simple thing. What most people don't realize is as a new franchisee you can negotiate a 3-6-month free period with the property owner, regardless of whether it's an existing agreement you are talking over or a new lease agreement.

Out of the hundreds of studios and gyms I have been a part of opening there have only been a handful of times that this has not been true.

So be sure to negotiate terms, and ask for 6 months. So, if they come back with a rebuttal you can drop to 3 months. This is a massive savings in the beginning. I want to get in for as little money as possible.

EQUIPMENT AGREEMENT AND TERMS

Equipment for a gym or studio with members can cost a small fortune. Which is why most choose to hire equipment or purchase through financing like you would your car. Often the terms are three to five years; some may be less or more, but I normally suggest making it the same length of time as your lease agreement in case you decide to move on, so it will be a smoother transition. Or if you sell it there will also be an easier transition.

There are many companies that offer this, but if you are buying an existing studio or gym, the current franchisee will more than likely have something in place.

Sometimes the franchisee will pay outright for equipment. The problem with that is that it could drastically increase the asking price for the gym. so I suggest looking for a studio or gym that uses a lease or financing company with equipment to keep costs down in the beginning. Then I can use profits from the business to cover the costs as we increase them.

If you do follow this system, which is buy low, increase the value of the business ten or twenty times, then sell, which I believe is the fastest way to build, the current franchisee will have an agreement in place for equipment.

So, the question is, when does that agreement finish? Is there a balloon at the end you will need to pay? What are the available options for upgrading? And so on...

Personally, I want the equipment lease to be up within six to eighteen months maximum, because when we get new equipment, it will give us an influx of new members, and current members will associate the change to new owners as being positive. At the same time, it gives us some breathing space to get some growth and iron out the kinks.

The biggest thing here really is, will this cost you money out of pocket? If the answer is yes, how much? To be honest I'm looking for an equipment agreement that will cost nothing, or a minimal upfront payment and an opportunity for new equipment in the near future, so that this expense will be covered by the new increased profits of the business. Without a balloon at the end.

PROFIT & LOSS STATEMENTS

The basis for buying or investing in any business is the financial reports. There is a balance sheet which is the assets versus liabilities. And the profit and loss statement, which is the total income versus total expenses monthly over the last financial year.

There is also a budget and financial forecast, as covered in the financial mastery chapter. To be honest, with this type of business and investment, all I'm really looking for is how the gym performed in the last 12–24 months. I want to see an accurate report of it broken down monthly, to determine if there are costs I can eliminate, and also to forecast my profits if I hit my growth target of members and personal training clients.

I would spend some time learning how to read financial statements, and in the meantime, have an accountant or other team who has experience with them look at them. Warren Buffet wrote a book called how to read financial statements; I highly recommend it.

With this system, I am building a portfolio of gyms. I buy them low and sell them high. Like the previous one, I can buy it for $45,000, increase it over 12-24 months and sell it at 10-20 times the original price, which is huge! Or use that capital growth as equity, not to mention reinvesting the profits.

I'm not looking for a successful gym, because If I buy a gym at $600,000–$800,000, there may not be as much room for growth. Sure, it may have the profits coming through, but I've got to spend a lot more money to get in. So, the risk to reward ratio is much higher. It's high risk and medium reward. I want low risk and high reward. You also have to take into consideration the cost of repaying the loan. This is why I generally aim to spend no more than $50,000–$100,000 on a studio or gym.

If you buy a $50,000 gym each year for 10 years and just follow this system you will turn that $500,000 over 10 years into $5,000,000–$10,000,000. That's a huge return on investment. Now I know they are just numbers, and just a forecast, but I have been doing this for a very long time, and this is the exact model we are using now to build a portfolio of investment gyms.

Warren Buffet says the number one rule of investing is to not lose money. Your worst case if you put a lot of money into it is bankruptcy. And your best case is a 7-figure gym. However, if you buy low, your worst case is you organize a repayment plan to the bank, spend none of your own money, and your best case is still the same. A 7-figure business. The gap is just much larger.

When reading these profit and loss statements, look for inconsistences in expenses, income and other variables that may stand out, then question them. My goal here is to ensure every month that the business is profitable, even if it's only a few dollars, as we will build it fast.

TEAM DYNAMICS & CULTURE

Before buying an investment gym I like to do a workout in it as a mystery shopper, so no one knows who I am. This way I can get a natural feel for the team culture, dynamics and work ethic.

I would rather buy an investment business without the extra cost and time of hiring a new team, especially management, although sometimes that may be necessary.

If your goal is to have a gym or studio that works without you, the team is super important. In fact I put my team before everything and anything else.

After doing your mystery shop, if you feel the culture or environment is a little toxic, it may be hard to re-create the culture you desire, and could take more time and energy than you want to spare to build a new team. The fact is, it will take time to build the culture you want. The further away the gym culture is from where you want it to be, the harder it will be.

As a rule, the larger the capital growth potential, the more work I'm prepared to do. For example, if I know I can build a gym to 15-20 times its turnover in under 2 years, I'm happy to spend 6 months building a strong team and culture.

If not, then I won't. I would rather excite the existing team with a new, big vision and have them feel like a partner, and use the existing team where possible. I focus on serving the team, then they can focus on serving the members. The greater I lead and serve the team, the greater they will serve and lead the members, and the better the culture will be.

BEGIN WITH THE END IN MIND

One of the biggest mistakes studio or gym owners make is they don't complete the vision of their business. What does it look like finished? You need to determine how many members, PTs, clients, staff it will have when it looks finished. Only then can you reverse engineer it.

In our business coaching program, we show fitness businesses exactly how to do this. An organizational structure, map, vision, mission, and more.

Be sure to take the time to determine:

1. What is your vision?
2. What is your mission?
3. What are your core values?

LAUNCHING A PT STUDIO

One of my favourite things to do is launching studios. We use a powerful three-week marketing campaign with an open week. To be honest it's kind of too big to include here, but if you become a client we will gladly share it. The goal by the end of the open week is to add at least six figures and be profitable. I have done this hundreds of times.

In the meantime, here is a video on the three things you need to launch and open your own studio; it's simple but powerful

→ https://youtu.be/mwAoi7Quggs

Bonus Chapter V
FREE TOOLS & RESOURCES

Below is a bunch of really cool tools and resources that are all free. I hope they add value to you on your journey to build a 7-figure fitness business...

Starter Kit for Online Personal Trainers -
freeonlineptstarterkit.com/

Facebook Marketing Planner for Personal Trainers -
ptsocialmediaplan.com/

YouTube Channel – Jason Grossman *(Please note for any links that for some reason do not work within this book to a video, ALL videos can be found on this channel within this book)*

10 Steps to Build a Successful Group Training Business Free eBook-
http://freegrouptrainingebook.com/

Advanced Communications for PTs Free Ebook –
https://advancedcommunciationspt.com/6-figure-pt-book

Get 2 Free Business Coaching Sessions –
https://freebusinesshealthcheck.com/

Free 14-Day Trial to Sales and Marketing Software –
https://clickfunnels.com/?cf_affiliate_id=641637&affiliate_id=641637

Facebook Fan page -
https://www.facebook.com/PersonalTrainersUnited/

Facebook VIP Group -
https://www.facebook.com/groups/251775854923163/

Facebook Community Group -
https://www.facebook.com/groups/PersonalTrainersofAustraliaUnited/

10

THE CLOSE

As I sit here and write this final chapter, I will admit this has taken a lot longer than I anticipated. It has taken hundreds of hours to write, read it and re-read it, because I really wanted to offer a book that delivered on its promise in the title. A bible for fitness business owners that covers everything it can in one book. For any and all Personal Trainers at any level with any desire or ambition. I really hope I have delivered on that, and I truly believe for the price of this book, the amount of value is truly phenomenal.

Does it cover everything? Definitely not. It's just one book, but the content in here is definitely enough to kick start your journey to build a 6- then 7-figure fitness business.

Besides, how much did you actually pay for this book? The content in here is worth hundreds of thousands if not more if you apply it!

Although this book, like any plan, won't guarantee your success, that is now up to you. I have done my job. I poured my heart and soul into this book and you, but that is all pointless if you don't stand up and take action. Remember why you are doing what you are doing and get to work!

I truly thank you for taking the time to read this entire book and hope you will take the time to implement everything within.

I believe those who apply the information in this book will achieve massive results. Even if you don't hit 7 figures, this will certainly catapult your success beyond what you were doing before reading this book.

Maybe the most important thing for you to do now is ask yourself the questions: if my business were a success, if it were finished, how would it look? If I could achieve anything in the fitness industry and I could not fail, what would I do?

Because then you can reverse engineer it from here and build it. Because hunger is the key to success. Don't be afraid to dream big. To own your own franchise, a portfolio of gyms or studios, a massive team that impacts thousands of lives or more. Do a world tour, be a renowned international coach, publish your book, launch a charity, an online business, generating millions and helping millions a year.

It is all possible if you have the courage to raise your standards and play a bigger game. You have so many skills and talents, so much knowledge, a story that can inspire millions, so I dare you to chase your dreams, serve and add value to others, and create a life for you and your family you dream of by creating a large fitness business that is scaled and creates financial freedom for you and your family. As you add value to the lives of thousands if not millions of people worldwide.

You don't just have to book yourself solid with sixty sessions a week and stay there. Sure, you may do that for a few years, but start thinking long term. PT is a stepping stone, you won't do it forever; so what steps will you take above and beyond PT? What dream will you relentlessly pursue until it becomes a reality? It's possible! But you have to make a decision right now—that even though you may not know how to do it, even though you may have doubts or fears, you are prepared to find the right people to guide you, to create a plan and align your psychology for success in the pursuit of your fitness dreams!

Get to work, take massive action and you can achieve anything!

You got this, it's time to run, it's time to go all in, it's time to make an impact! Now is the time to take massive action, and transform your dream of a 7-figure fitness business into a reality.

How badly do you want it?

Jason Grossman
#GSD

TESTIMONIALS

From since I remember, all I have ever wanted was to help people and relieve them from pain and struggle, and if I had the resources to do so I would!

I was brought up in a very dysfunctional family. Moved out of home at the age of 14 and was completely independent by 16. You name struggle in nearly every situation and I have mostly likely lived it. I guess this is why I feel so good helping others through struggle.

During this period, I became very overweight and depressed and one day I put my foot down and did something about it. I lost over 50kg in 6 months and felt the instant relief physically and mentally and knew this is what I wanted to do is help others do the same.

I did my studies and pursued my passion in fitness...

A few years went on...I grinded 80+ hour work weeks to try pick up clients and thrive, to be the face of the gym. I have been a personal trainer for over 5 years now and have had the pleasure of helping hundreds of individuals physically and mentally.

I hit a point where I couldn't manage everything and hit a wall, so I looked for help. That's where I found Jason Grossman.

I can count the number of weeks on my 2 hands and business doubled. And after a short while it tripled. Had tragic family issues, lost my whole business, and STILL managed to pick it back up again with the help of Jason.

I have built a 6-figure fitness business with a team of trainers and on my way to unlocking the $250,000 a year club which, with the help of Jason, I know I will hit! Not only have learnt intense sales and marketing but most importantly the psychology and how to really connect with people.

I highly recommend Quantum Fitness Marketing if you want to grow scale and automate your fitness business and explode to a level you never thought was possible.

Thanks, Jason, for all your help.
Daniel Rousso – Melbourne Australia

My journey into the Health, Wellness and Fitness Industry began just over 20 years now, since arriving in Australia from New Zealand. I absolutely loved it, however after 10 years of being in the industry, and at the age of 41, I became burnt out and suffered from Adrenal Fatigue sending my body into hormonal chaos, exhausted and putting on weight. This meant giving up my beloved Personal Training and passion to focus on healing myself, which took me two long years and lots of study on hormones and menopause, nutrition, exercise and psychology after 40. I became an NLP Practitioner and hypnotherapist in that time.

Out of a harrowing time in my life, Menofitness was born. It was during this time I thought... if I was a fit, strong and healthy PT and felt so bad, how did other over-40 female PT's feel going through hormonal changes and more importantly how did they train and educate their 40+ female clients? So, I created an online Menofitness course that was registered in 5 different countries and 7 different fitness organisations, and had the pleasure of educating over 1200 PT's on menopause and fitness, and from there developed my signature program designed to help Personal Trainers help their menopausal clients. At that time, even though my business was surviving, it was by no means thriving.

With the help of Jason Grossman from Quantum Fitness Marketing, and the amazing strategies, tools and coaching, we are now thriving. I have been able to grow my online fitness business to 6-figures, to the stage where I am so busy that I now employ 2 more coaches to help with the demand, a telemarketer to manage the abundance of leads, and am leveraging even more through my menopause program for PT's.

I truly believe that this is just the beginning of something huge and my vision to help 1 million women 40+ live the life they so rightly deserve is unfolding. My heart is filled with absolute gratitude to Jason for the patience, support, knowledge and opportunity he has given me. Due to QFM, my vision is now possible.

Lyn Miller – Gold Coast Australia

In September 2017, I had just finished my Master's degree in strength and conditioning and I turned my focus to my personal training business, which was doing ok. I first came across QFM at a tough time in my life, we had a year and a half's council tax to pay inside 4 months due to an error in the system which led us to believe we were exempt with me being a student at the time, this equated to £2,550 sterling.

On top of that I had just lost my ability to drive and was going through a legal case due to a technical error on my part which meant that I had been stopped driving without car insurance. The fines from this case were £2,231 sterling across the same 4-month period. There was a total of £1,500 to pay on the 11th of December 2017 and that was before one present was bought or the boat paid for my partner, daughter and I to get to Ireland to see the rest of my family for Christmas. This was only my daughter's 2nd Christmas, so would be a massive deal if we didn't make it, both to myself and my family.

I was pretty stressed out and really wasn't sure how I would get through it all. I had seen Jason's book on how to build a 6-figure PT business online and it was given away for free; I thought it can't hurt to have a look and see what this book had to offer. It was an inspiring story and made me realize my situation wasn't that bad, and it gave me some useful marketing strategies. I then received the FB message offering me two free business coaching calls; this was a no brainer, I could use all the help I could get.

So, I took the call with Simon Finch who is now my business coach, we discussed my situation and he pleaded with me to trust him and come on the Christmas marketing workshop run by Jason. He said it would make me $5,000-10,000 (£2,500-5000) before Christmas. I was so shocked that he believed this and said it with such conviction that I had to give it a crack. After all, it only actually cost $200 (£100); thought it's a relatively small risk for a massive reward. That month I made £6,300 following the strategies in the marketing plan and some with my own twist on their ideas.

I am still working with Simon on my business, we are now in May 2018, and I am due to open my own PT facility on July 1st. I am crazy excited to finally execute my dream idea of creating a facility with all the best specialists in Training, Nutrition, Physiotherapy and CBT. I have done a lot of reading in the last year and have altered my mindset a lot to reach success. However, if it wasn't for Simon, Jason and the QFM team, I would not have had the belief and tools necessary to realize my dream. I am eternally grateful, and I will go all the way to the top with QFM to the millionaires' group and beyond. I have 3 years to be a millionaire by the time I am 30. With the help of the QFM team, there is no doubt in my mind I will achieve this because I will help so many people on my way. Now I have hit 6-figures, next step is the $250,000K Club and that's POUNDS!

Tiarnán Carlin – England, United Kingdom

I became a qualified PT in September 2016. Prior to that I worked in a leadership position for a period of 10 years for a couple of different companies. I had been a keen trainer for years and taught myself a lot about nutrition. I had always been drawn to health and fitness articles and websites and, just a couple of years ago, I finally figured out what I needed to do with my life. I made the big jump to become an entrepreneur in the fitness industry with a goal to help thousands of people live healthier and happier lives.

To be honest, I had no idea what I was in for. I started at a Goodlife Health Club in Adelaide in October 2016. I did ok for the first 10 months (or maybe we should call it "surviving" for 10 months). On average, I was making about $1000 per week. Take away the $317 gym rent, tax, then pay the mortgage and household bills, let's be honest, I really was just surviving.

My friend and business partner, Ethan Schoepf, and I worked together to find marketing companies to help us grow our brand online. We found Quantum Fitness Marketing through Facebook and I spoke to Jason Grossman about helping me grow my business through social media. He said he could absolutely help me do that, but first I need to maximize my potential in the gym.

Jason left me in the very capable hands of my personal business coach, Rhys Margan. Rhys has been an amazing coach. Rhys has helped me re-shape my mindset from what I thought was possible, which was limiting my potential, to what I never imagined was possible. Four months of coaching with Rhys, I was fully booked in the gym, my business grew to over $150K, I had contracted a trainer to help me deliver sessions, and my goal now is to help change over 1 million people's lives to live healthier happier lifestyles, and only now starting to seriously grow my fitness business online.

Contacting Quantum Fitness Marketing was the best decision I have made for my business to date. Without Jason and Rhys' help, I would be just another passionate fitness pro chasing my tail in the business world, not maximizing my potential. I do not want to know where I'd be without the help from QFM – But now I do know the direction I am going. Let's just say, this is just the beginning ☺

Jenna May – Adelaide, Australia.

I was a sporty kid growing up; I played most sports going. My chosen sport was Rugby league, I played this semi-professionaly in New Zealand and as a full-time profession in the English Superleague for three years. Once that career finished, I realised I had some skills in training myself, which I loved, so when I came home to NZ I studied at AUT, and I became a certified PT that same year, 1994. Wow, that's 24 years ago now!

My business, The Power Of Two Limited, has been pretty solid for most of those years, making gross somewhere between 80 and 150k annually. I opened RAW Ener-CHI, with my business partner, Joe Lewis, on 1 February 2018. We wanted to truly impact the community that we opened the center in.

I searched for a business coach and found Jason Grossman. I checked him out and saw that Jason was having strong successes with his clients. I committed to the Quantum coaching system and was introduced to Simon (the freak) Finch. Although I have been in the industry for many more years than Simon, and even Jason, these guys had moved on in the industry. Businesswise they have tools that I did not even know existed for PT businesses!

Simon has been incredibly helpful in growing my business! He has shared mulitple tools to gear up my business for growth and success. I am booked solidly , with 40+ weekly one hour sessions and my business partner is at 30+ weekly. The fact is, I'm too busy now, so Simon has worked with me on a plan to hire trainers to grow my business further!

We employed our first trainer just last week, I'm handing some of my sessions onto the new trainer and will reduce my hours working in the business down to 30 hours weekly. This will free-up time for me to work on the business rather than in it, and to duplicate!

I am pleased to say that Simon has not only helped me with a planning strategy, the guy also celebrates my successes just about as much as I do! What this all means from a business perspective is, with just Joe and myself working in the business, we easily crack the 250K milestone! Within 6 months, we will be in the 500k zone! We will then open our second center and repeat the process, until we have opened an international High performance center, with a swimming pool, movement studio, Olympic lifting studio and ufc type training facility! We are rocking it!

Thanks, Simon and Jason, for your coaching and support, very grateful!

Rod Fielder – Auckland, New Zealand

Just over a year ago, I was scrolling through Facebook and saw a post from Jason Grossman about how he helped a PT build a 6-figure fitness business in less than 8 weeks. Not believing this was even possible, I sent a PM to the person he coached, and they reassured me that it was, in fact, true...

I then made the decision to reach out to Jason and get some coaching. At the time, I was working in a job I hated and really wanted to get back into the health and fitness industry, so I could start helping people and make a difference and impact lives. With the guidance of Jason and Rhys, I was able to quit my job in 4 weeks and build a 6-figure business in 6 weeks!!!

In just over one year, I was able to build to 250k and now have two trainers working for me. And I now have the honour of working for QFM and helping other trainers to build their fitness business up as a business coach. I am excited to work toward the next rank of 500k and believe I will achieve that goal this year.

Increasing my income has allowed me to do more things, including personal development. In fact, as I write this I am at a 6-day Tony Robbins personal development seminar. Getting a passive income whilst I am away. In June, I will be flying to Sydney to Learn NLP from a master practitioner and further my coaching skills.

My new goal is to be the best coach from QFM and help other passionate personal trainers build faster than I did. I am excited to learn and grow from the best in the industry and be a part of this amazing team of coaches ☺

If you are reading this and have never tried having a business coach to take it to the next level, then I highly recommend you give it a go! It's been the best thing I have ever done, and I am now living my destiny and doing what I was born to do.

Sincerely
James Trenow – Perth, Western Australia

My journey into the health and fitness scene started just over 8 years ago in Adelaide, Australia. At the time, I was 16-years-old and had my first experience doing weights at school in PE. I was always really skinny and hated it; I remember weighing not much over 60kg, at over 6ft, and was one of the weakest kids in the class. In that moment, I made a decision to do something about it and have never looked back.

This was ultimately the determining factor in me become a PT some 4 years later. I had seen what a massive difference putting on muscle had done to my confidence and overall happiness. I knew if I could do it, then I could help other people achieve the same thing.

After doing the appropriate study to become a personal trainer, I landed myself a job at a big box gym as a rental trainer. I had my hopes set on the stars and thought it wouldn't be long before I was booked out and making lots of money. Unfortunately, just over a year later, I wasn't in much of a better position financially than when I first started. I had a handful of clients but was always struggling week to week to pay the rent at the gym and to afford all my bills at home. Like a lot of personal trainers out there I knew what I was doing in the gym, but I didn't know how to market or sell my services.

This whole experience was disheartening, but I didn't give up. When my contract ended at this gym I began working for a Mobile Personal training business. This prompted me to then start my own Mobile business as I liked the structure and idea of training people from their homes.

Less than a year later, I came across Jason and Quantum Fitness Marketing on Facebook and arranged our first coaching call. 18 months on, with the guidance of Jason, I have built a team of 5 trainers all across Adelaide, and I am currently making more than 250k per year! I was also lucky enough to become a business coach for QFM, and I am now helping personal trainers in 4 countries as their business coach to follow their dreams and our systems to build to 6-figures plus.

I do truly believe that this is only the beginning, and I know that if I stick to the process the next 18 months I will hit 7-figures and beyond! I can't thank Jason enough for the amazing opportunity he has given to myself and the other coaches, not to mention the thousands of personal trainers that have gone through this program.

Lachy Black – Adelaide, Australia

My health and fitness journey started about 6 years ago. In my late teens and early twenties, I got myself heavily addicted to drugs and alcohol and basically destroyed my life. Lost every job I could get, got kicked out of the houses I was living in, lost my real friends and ended up stealing and selling to fuel my drug habit.

Long story short, I found health and fitness and began to turn my life around. Through relentless physical and mental development, I was able to pull myself out of the hole I had dug and addict myself to something positive in life, using my unique knowledge and experiences to help others live healthier and happier lives.

4 years on from my turn around, I started studying to become a personal trainer. 2 years after that I qualified and started up a free outdoor boot camp on Saturdays. I had so much passion and desire that people flocked to my Saturday sessions. I had 20-25 people coming after 2-3 months. This is when I decided to start up paid weekday classes before and after my full-time job. As soon as I started charging for my services, everyone disappeared…It was frustrating because I knew I could help them but didn't know how to make them realise it.

After a few weeks of failing at running a business, I started to look for a way out. I came across Jason Grossman the author of this book. We got on a call together and I said, "HELP ME!" Jason took me on as a business coaching client and the rest is history. Through his program and guidance, I was able to build to 100k a year income in just 4 weeks after joining a big box gym! This absolutely blew my mind that it could be done so fast. With my sights set on success, I continued to build.

I now run a multiple 6-figure business. I am a business coach to over 20 fitness business owners in 6 different countries with Quantum Fitness Marketing. I have helped clients build to 100k-250k and even had one client surpass me by building to 500k+ a year.

Finding Jason and joining this amazing community has completely revolutionized my life. I will be eternally grateful for the opportunities I've been given. The beautiful thing is: this is just the beginning.

As great as all this is, the thing I am most excited about is this year I'm fulfilling my dream of launching a charity organization, with the guidance of Jason, that will help less fortunate people world-wide and truly make an impact.

Rhys Margan – Perth, Western Australia

Just under two years ago, I made a decision to hit the reset button, forget everything I had ever done career wise, and to re-train in a completely new industry. Little did I know that it was soon to be the best decision of my life, up until that point. I had always admired Personal Trainers and loved the flexibility they had to manage their own schedule and to live their life helping others achieve their dream physique and level of fitness.

I made the long trip from the UK, over 6 years ago now, equipped with my degree in Geology, in search of work in the mining industry. After many twists and turns in Perth, WA, I eventually moved up to Darwin, NT, where I became a member of an outdoor group fitness class and this is where my spark and passion was ignited. After spending a few years in Darwin and gaining my qualifications, the next chapter was to be made in Melbourne, VIC, where I began working as a self-employed Fitness Business Owner.

I hit the ground running and got off to what I thought at the time was a great start. It was then I was recommended by a friend in the industry to speak to Jason Grossman from QFM and the rest, as they say, is history.

In a matter of weeks, I catapulted my business to over $100k, then onwards to $150k+ and could not believe what was happening and the speed at which it was. In the closing weeks of 2017, I hit the lucrative $250k milestone and became the busiest QFM Coach, which I see as an achievement of all my hard work and dedication to others.

Along the way, there have been two significant moments that have been milestones for not only my achievements but also my personal development as an entrepreneur. The rank of $100k and onwards from $200k to $250k. I can only say that the hard work and consistency really does pay off, but these two milestones truly tested me and molded me into the person I am today. Now I am blessed to be a business coach with Jason and QFM, coaching PTs in 6 countries to build their business.

As a coach now with QFM, my goal is to continue to help the masses in the industry and to get them into continually stronger positions than they are at present, in turn, impacting thousands of lives. In my first few months as coach, I have been fortunate enough to take multiple individuals to $100k+ and have also helped others achieve the $250k mark too!

Anything is possible, and if you ever get the chance to read this and are thinking about making a decision to make your fitness business explode, then you are certainly in the right place.

Simon Finch – Melbourne, Australia.

Wanting to become a personal trainer stemmed from my own desire and struggles to earn and to maintain a fit looking physique. It was after injuries I sustained in 2010 that I discovered and adopted the High Intensity Training Method. It proved to be a significant contribution to my physical progress and launched me into a successful career as a personal trainer.

Now, 8 years in the industry, I have established myself as a tough no-nonsense trainer that uses scientifically proven methods and dedication to achieve life-changing results for my clients. 3 years into my career, I was blessed with the opportunity to purchase the training studio I was then employed at. This was an opportunity that I took full advantage of. With a full-functioning facility at my disposal, I was able to achieve a six-figure income my first year, achieving just under 200k. I continued my success achieving just over 200k my second year. In my third year, with investments into a new website, and focusing on search engine optimization, I grew to 260k. I was astounded by the growth and thankful for my success. This all, mind you, without a business degree and no formal marketing education.

After suffering a stroke in early 2018, I knew that if I wanted to take my business growth to the next level I needed help. I decided to scour Facebook looking for experts. Finally, an expert reached out to me. A guy from Australia by the name of Jason Grossman. After an enlightening and informative call, a call that resonated with me, I joined. From there my business became a rocket ship. I was being provided strategies that I had never even considered—strategies not only for my business but for me personally. I was provided the tools and mindset to take financial control of my life. Before I knew it, I achieved my 500k badge with my sights now set on accomplishing a million-dollar-a-year fitness business.

With Jason striving to make all those who follow him a millionaire, I jumped in completely open minded and ready to learn. Now, in May of 2018, I have the honor to call myself a Quantum Fitness Marketing Business Coach, representing the United States. I look forward to helping my fellow personal trainers worldwide accomplish their financial dreams as I have been able to.

Thank you to my coaches Rhys Margan and Jason Grossman for all that you do.

Dustin Wenzel – Michigan, United States of America.